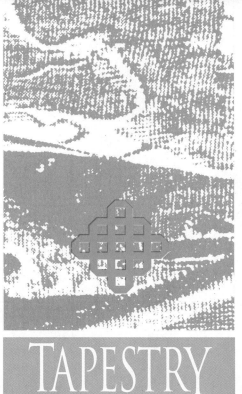

TAPESTRY

STUDY SKILLS
FOR
ACADEMIC
SUCCESS

TAPESTRY

The **Tapestry** program of language materials is based on the concepts presented in *The Tapestry of Language Learning: The Individual in the Communicative Classroom* by Robin C. Scarcella & Rebecca L. Oxford.

Each title in this program focuses on:

Individual learner strategies and instruction

The relatedness of skills

Ongoing self-assessment

Authentic material as input

Theme-based learning linked to task-based instruction

Attention to all aspects of communicative competence

TAPESTRY

STUDY SKILLS FOR ACADEMIC SUCCESS

Cheryl Wecksler

Heinle & Heinle Publishers
An International Thomson
Publishing Company
Boston, Massachusetts, 02116, USA

ITP

The publication of *Study Skills for Academic Success* was directed by the members of the Heinle & Heinle Global Innovations Publishing Team:

Elizabeth Holthaus, Global Innovations Team Leader
David C. Lee, Editorial Director
John F. McHugh, Market Development Director
Lisa McLaughlin, Production Services Coordinator

Also participating in the publication of this program were:

Director of Production: Elizabeth Holthaus
Publisher: Stanley J. Galek
Assistant Editor: Kenneth Mattsson
Manufacturing Coordinator: Mary Beth Hennebury
Full Service Project Manager/Compositor: PC&F, Inc.
Interior Design: Maureen Lauran
Cover Design: Maureen Lauran

Manufactured in the United States of America

ISBN: 0-8384-3958-6

Heinle & Heinle Publishers is an International Thomson Publishing Company.

10 9 8 7 6 5 4 3 2 1

To Howard

WELCOME TO TAPESTRY

*E*nter the world of Tapestry! Language learning can be seen as an ever-developing tapestry woven with many threads and colors. The elements of the tapestry are related to different language skills like listening and speaking, reading and writing; the characteristics of the teachers; the desires, needs, and backgrounds of the students; and the general second language development process. When all these elements are working together harmoniously, the result is a colorful, continuously growing tapestry of language competence of which the student and the teacher can be proud.

This volume is part of the Tapestry program for students of English as a second language (ESL) at levels from beginning to "bridge" (which follows the advanced level and prepares students to enter regular postsecondary programs along with native English speakers). Tapestry levels include:

Beginning
Low Intermediate
High Intermediate
Low Advanced
High Advanced
Bridge

Because the Tapestry program provides a unified theoretical and pedagogical foundation for all its components, you can optimally use all the Tapestry student books in a coordinated fashion as an entire curriculum of materials. (They will be published from 1993 to 1996 with further editions likely thereafter.) Alternatively, you can decide to use just certain Tapestry volumes, depending on your specific needs.

Tapestry is primarily designed for ESL students at postsecondary institutions in North America. Some want to learn ESL for academic or career advancement, others for social and personal reasons. Tapestry builds directly on all these motivations. Tapestry stimulates learners to do their best. It enables learners to use English naturally and to develop fluency as well as accuracy.

Tapestry Principles

The following principles underlie the instruction provided in all of the components of the Tapestry program.

EMPOWERING LEARNERS

Language learners in Tapestry classrooms are active and increasingly responsible for developing their English language skills and related cultural abilities. This self direction leads to better, more rapid learning. Some cultures virtually train their students to be passive in the classroom, but Tapestry weans them from passivity by providing exceptionally high interest materials, colorful and motivating activities, personalized self-reflection tasks, peer tutoring and other forms of cooperative learning, and powerful learning strategies to boost self direction in learning.

The empowerment of learners creates refreshing new roles for teachers, too. The teacher serves as facilitator, co-communicator, diagnostician, guide, and helper. Teachers are set free to be more creative at the same time their students become more autonomous learners.

HELPING STUDENTS IMPROVE THEIR LEARNING STRATEGIES

Learning strategies are the behaviors or steps an individual uses to enhance his or her learning. Examples are taking notes, practicing, finding a conversation partner, analyzing words, using background knowledge, and controlling anxiety. Hundreds of such strategies have been identified. Successful language learners use language learning strategies that are most effective for them given their particular learning style, and they put them together smoothly to fit the needs of a given language task. On the other hand, the learning strategies of less successful learners are a desperate grab-bag of ill-matched techniques.

All learners need to know a wide range of learning strategies. All learners need systematic practice in choosing and applying strategies that are relevant for various learning needs. Tapestry is one of the only ESL programs that overtly weaves a comprehensive set of learning strategies into language activities in all its volumes. These learning strategies are arranged in eight broad categories throughout the Tapestry books:

Forming concepts
Personalizing
Remembering new material
Managing your learning
Understanding and using emotions
Overcoming limitations
Testing Hypotheses
Learning with Others

The most useful strategies are sometimes repeated and flagged with a note, "It Works! Learning Strategy . . ." to remind students to use a learning strategy they have already encountered. This recycling reinforces the value of learning strategies and provides greater practice.

RECOGNIZING AND HANDLING LEARNING STYLES EFFECTIVELY

Learners have different learning styles (for instance, visual, auditory, hands- on; reflective, impulsive; analytic, global; extroverted, introverted; closure-oriented, open). Particularly in an ESL setting, where students come from vastly different cultural backgrounds, learning styles differences abound and can cause "style conflicts."

Unlike most language instruction materials, Tapestry provides exciting activities specifically tailored to the needs of students with a large range of learning styles. You can use any Tapestry volume with the confidence that the activities and materials are intentionally geared for many different styles. Insights from the latest educational and psychological research undergird this style-nourishing variety.

OFFERING AUTHENTIC, MEANINGFUL COMMUNICATION

Students need to encounter language that provides authentic, meaningful communication. They must be involved in real-life communication tasks that cause them to *want* and *need* to read, write, speak, and listen to English. Moreover, the tasks—to be most effective—must be arranged around themes relevant to learners.

Themes like family relationships, survival in the educational system, personal health, friendships in a new country, political changes, and protection of the environment are all valuable to ESL learners. Tapestry focuses on topics like these. In every Tapestry volume, you will see specific content drawn from very broad areas such as home life, science and technology, business, humanities, social sciences, global issues, and multiculturalism. All the themes are real and important, and they are fashioned into language tasks that students enjoy.

At the advanced level, Tapestry also includes special books each focused on a single broad theme. For instance, there are two books on business English, two on English for science and technology, and two on academic communication and study skills.

UNDERSTANDING AND VALUING DIFFERENT CULTURES

Many ESL books and programs focus completely on the "new" culture, that is, the culture which the students are entering. The implicit message is that ESL students should just learn about this target culture, and there is no need to understand their own culture better or to find out about the cultures of their international classmates. To some ESL students, this makes them feel their own culture is not valued in the new country.

Tapestry is designed to provide a clear and understandable entry into North American culture. Nevertheless, the Tapestry Program values *all* the cultures found in the ESL classroom. Tapestry students have constant opportunities to become "culturally fluent" in North American culture while they are learning English, but they also have the chance to think about the cultures of their classmates and even understand their home culture from different perspectives.

INTEGRATING THE LANGUAGE SKILLS

Communication in a language is not restricted to one skill or another. ESL students are typically expected to learn (to a greater or lesser degree) all four language skills: reading, writing, speaking, and listening. They are also expected to develop strong grammatical competence, as well as becoming socioculturally sensitive and knowing what to do when they encounter a "language barrier."

Research shows that multi-skill learning is more effective than isolated-skill learning, because related activities in several skills provide reinforcement and refresh the learner's memory. Therefore, Tapestry integrates all the skills. A given Tapestry volume might highlight one skill, such as reading, but all other skills are also included to support and strengthen overall language development.

However, many intensive ESL programs are divided into classes labeled according to one skill (Reading Comprehension Class) or at most two skills (Listening/Speaking Class or Oral Communication Class). The volumes in the Tapestry Program can easily be used to fit this traditional format, because each volume clearly identifies its highlighted or central skill(s).

Grammar is interwoven into all Tapestry volumes. However, there is also a separate reference book for students, *The Tapestry Grammar,* and a Grammar Strand composed of grammar "work-out" books at each of the levels in the Tapestry Program.

Other Features of the Tapestry Program

PILOT SITES

It is not enough to provide volumes full of appealing tasks and beautiful pictures. Users deserve to know that the materials have been pilot-tested. In many ESL series, pilot testing takes place at only a few sites or even just in the classroom of the author. In contrast, Heinle & Heinle Publishers have developed a network of Tapestry Pilot Test Sites throughout North America. At this time, there are approximately 40 such sites, although the number grows weekly. These sites try out the materials and provide suggestions for revisions. They are all actively engaged in making Tapestry the best program possible.

AN OVERALL GUIDEBOOK

To offer coherence to the entire Tapestry Program and especially to offer support for teachers who want to understand the principles and practice of Tapestry, we have written a book entitled, *The Tapestry of Language Learning. The Individual in the Communicative Classroom* (Scarcella and Oxford, published in 1992 by Heinle & Heinle).

A Last Word

We are pleased to welcome you to Tapestry! We use the Tapestry principles every day, and we hope these principles—and all the books in the Tapestry Program— provide you the same strength, confidence, and joy that they give us. We look forward to comments from both teachers and students who use any part of the Tapestry Program.

Rebecca L. Oxford
University of Alabama
Tuscaloosa, Alabama

Robin C. Scarcella
University of California at Irvine
Irvine, California

PREFACE

Study Skills for Academic Success is a high-intermediate to low-advanced textbook intended for students who plan to enter American colleges and universities. The purpose of this text is to introduce students to the type of work they will have to do in a typical university program and to provide them with the skills and strategies necessary to succeed in the system. Students will learn to take advantage of university services and use the university library. They will read from academic textbooks, listen to related lectures, and then take quizzes based on the readings and lectures. The chapters build upon three basic academic skills—reading textbooks and other types of academic writing, listening to lectures and taking notes, and taking tests. The students learn individual skills and then put all of these skills together as they will have to do in the university.

Authentic material is always used in this book. The readings are unsimplified chapters from textbooks and other sources with which university students must become familiar. Students listen to and take notes from academic lectures and discussions. Writing skills include answering essay exam questions, summarizing, and reacting to the readings, lectures, and discussion topics. Speaking skills focus on asking for clarification in an academic setting, participating in class discussions, and giving an oral presentation. Students also acquire both objective and subjective test-taking skills.

Achieving academic success is an active process. A variety of practice exercises follow each skill presented in the text. All exercises are student centered. All language skills are integrated. *Study Skills for Academic Success* focuses on the responsibility that each student must assume in order to succeed in an American university. Many of the exercises require the students to work independently or with a partner and to take the initiative to figure out how to complete a task. By enabling students to work on their own and to take responsibility for their academic performance, *Study Skills for Academic Success* helps them make the transition between the ESL classroom and the American university.

To the Instructor

Each chapter begins with a brief list of objectives and discussion questions that prepare the students for the upcoming material. The exercises all provide practical, hands-on experience that enables students to develop academic skills in preparation for the university. All chapters end with a summary that divides the skills presented into two groups: **ON YOUR OWN** and **IN CLASS.** In this way, students can see the amount of personal responsibility they must assume in order to succeed in the university.

Textbook readings are in Appendix A. In content-based courses and adjunct courses, the instructors will provide their own course readings, lectures, and quizzes. The class can focus on the skills presented in the textbook and will not be distracted by the reading passages.

Appendix B contains a glossary of university and library terminology. This essential vocabulary is used throughout the book. Students can use the glossary as a reference source.

The Instructor's Manual includes an answer key, chapter notes, the lecture scripts, and chapter tests. A sample syllabus and evaluation forms are also included in the manual.

Acknowledgments

I wish to thank Lynne Barsky, Developmental Editor, for her helpful assistance and advice. Jocelyn Steer provided me with many useful suggestions and a great deal of encouragement while she was working on *Strategies for Academic Communication,* the advanced study skills textbook for this series. In addition, I would like to thank Sandra G. Carrettin (University of Houston), Philip Less (University of Arkansas, Little Rock), Robin Scarcella (University of California, Irvine), Rebecca Oxford (University of Alabama), Robert P. Fox (St. Michael's College), and Lida Baker (University of California, Los Angeles) for their helpful comments during the development of this book. I would also like to extend my thanks to Elaine Hall and Shirley Simmons at PC&F for their work in the production of this book.

Cheryl Wecksler

CONTENTS

1 Beginning the Academic Year　1

INTRODUCTION	2
TAKING RESPONSIBILITY	2
LEARNING YOUR WAY AROUND	3
GETTING HELP ON CAMPUS	4
SETTING GOALS FOR YOURSELF	6
DEVELOPING GOOD STUDY HABITS	7
USING A COLLEGE CATALOG	8
USING A COMPREHENSIVE CLASS SCHEDULE	12
UNDERSTANDING THE COURSE SYLLABUS	14
DROPPING AND ADDING COURSES	15
MANAGING YOUR TIME	15
SUMMARY	20

2 Using the Library　21

INTRODUCTION	22
LEARNING YOUR WAY AROUND THE LIBRARY	22
LEARNING BASIC LIBRARY SKILLS	25
Understanding the Library of Congress System of Classification	26
USING THE GENERAL REFERENCE AREA	28
Using Different Reference Sources	29
FINDING BOOKS	31
Alphabetizing	31
Using the Library of Congress Subject Headings (LCSH)	34
Locating Books by Subject, Author, or Title	35
Locating Books in the Stacks by Call Number	39

FINDING JOURNAL ARTICLES 40

FINDING NEWSPAPER
ARTICLES 43

LOCATING PERIODICALS
IN THE LIBRARY 44

WORKING IN THE REFERENCE
AREA 45

WORKING IN THE LIBRARY 46

SUMMARY 51

3 *Reading, Notetaking, and Taking an Objective Test* 53

INTRODUCTION 54

ORGANIZING YOUR COURSE
MATERIAL 54

READING ACADEMIC WRITING 56
Recognizing the Topic, Main Idea, and
Details in a Paragraph 56
Recognizing Signal Words 57
Reading and Underlining in
Your Textbook 60
Making Notations in the Margins 61

USING THE SQ3R METHOD OF
READING 62

TAKING LECTURE NOTES 66
Filling in the Gaps After a Lecture 71

PARAPHRASING 72
Studying Your Notes 76

PREPARING FOR AN
OBJECTIVE TEST 77
Reading Directions and Budgeting
Your Time on an Objective Test 81

TAKING AN OBJECTIVE TEST 82

SUMMARY 83

4 *Reading, Notetaking, and Taking an Essay Test* 85

INTRODUCTION 86
Keeping Up with Your Work 86
Reading and Preparing Study Notes 87

SUMMARIZING 87

REFINING YOUR LECTURE
NOTES 92

IMPROVING YOUR MEMORY 93

GETTING INVOLVED IN CLASS
DISCUSSIONS 96

SYNTHESIZING COURSE
MATERIAL 98

PREPARING FOR AN
ESSAY TEST 100
Reading and Understanding Essay
Test Questions 100
Budgeting Your Time on an Essay Test 101
Writing Essay Test Answers 103
Editing Essay Test Answers 106
Guessing Test Questions in Advance 106
Preparing Practice Answers 107

TAKING AN ESSAY TEST 107

SUMMARY 108

5 *Working on a Group Project* 109

INTRODUCTION 110

WORKING WITH A GROUP 110
Understanding the Assignment 111
Meeting Deadlines 112

CHOOSING A TOPIC 113
Brainstorming 114
Writing a Thesis Statement 117

USING BOOKS AS REFERENCES 118

WRITING ONE-SENTENCE SUMMARIES 119

KNOWING YOUR AUDIENCE 121

THINKING CRITICALLY 122

ARGUING PERSUASIVELY 124

COMPLETING THE PROJECT 126
Presenting Your Project to the Class 128

SETTING PRIORITIES 128

ANALYZING YOUR ACADEMIC STRENGTHS AND WEAKNESSES 129

SUMMARY 131

Appendix A 133

TEXTBOOK CHAPTER FOR CHAPTER 3 134

TEXTBOOK CHAPTER FOR CHAPTER 4 148

TEXTBOOK CHAPTER FOR CHAPTER 5 163

Appendix B 175

GLOSSARY OF UNIVERSITY TERMINOLOGY 176

GLOSSARY OF LIBRARY TERMINOLOGY 179

Beginning the Academic Year

In this chapter you will:

- think about taking responsibility for your academic success.
- learn where to go to get help on campus.
- analyze your goals and study habits.
- use a college catalog.
- understand a course syllabus and the requirements of a course.
- manage your course load and your time.

The beginning of the academic year in a new college or university is always an intimidating experience. It's helpful to become familiar with the school and the services that it offers before you begin your classes. You'll be able to concentrate on your work more fully once your classes begin. In this way, you can get your semester off to a strong start.

Discuss the following questions with your classmates.

1. How did you feel when you arrived at this school? Were you lonely and confused, or did you feel comfortable and confident? Explain.
2. Do you feel that you have a clear set of goals? What are they?
3. Do you know where to go on campus to get answers to your questions? Give some examples of campus services with which you are familiar.
4. Do you think you have good study habits? Why or why not?
5. Do you have trouble keeping up with your school work? Explain.

TAKING RESPONSIBILITY

In college, you are on your own, and you have to take the initiative to solve your own problems. Many people on campus are ready and willing to help you, but you have to know where to go to get their assistance. If you are on a large campus, learn your way around right away. Check the information center and bulletin boards for information about tours and orientation activities for new students. You should learn your way around campus and about services offered to students before your classes begin. You'll be too busy after your classes start.

EXERCISE 1.1

Directions: If you are on a large campus, get a campus map. If you were involved in an orientation program, you might find a map in your orientation packet. If not, use the map in your college catalog or pick one up at the information center on campus. Locate the following places on the map:

The building where most of your classes are held
The building where your program's offices are located
The library (or libraries)
The cafeteria (or cafeterias)
Student health services
Administrative offices
The foreign student advisor's office
The bookstore
The gymnasium
Recreational facilities (pool, tennis courts, etc.)
The dormitory (or dormitories)
The information center or information booths
The parking office

If you can't find these places on your map, ask your instructor for help.

EXERCISE 1.2

Directions: Once you have located these places on the map, go for a walk on campus to find each of the locations listed in Exercise 1.1. While you are walking around campus, answer the following questions and complete the following tasks.

1. Are your English language classes held in the same buildings that the regular university classes use, or does your program use a separate building?
2. Go into the library. What do you see in the entrance area? Are there any brochures or maps in this area? If so, pick up a map of the library.
3. Go into the student health services office. Are there any brochures or pamphlets available? If so, pick up one or two which you think would be interesting or useful.
4. What time do the cafeterias open in the morning? Are they open on the week-end?
5. Look around the cafeteria and the bulletin board areas. Can you find any brochures, pamphlets, flyers, or newspapers nearby? Pick up anything that looks interesting to you.
6. Go into the bookstore. What is sold there other than books?
7. What kinds of recreational facilities are on campus? Are rules and regulations posted outside these facilities? What are they?

While you are walking around the campus, you'll notice that there is information all around you. Pick up some of the brochures and pamphlets that you find and read them. Read the information posted on bulletin boards throughout the campus, and pick up the student newspaper on a regular basis. Important information about services and events on campus is available in many places. Get into the habit of looking for this information.

EXERCISE 1.3

Directions: After you return, report to the class on what you learned on campus. Look at the printed material that you picked up. Choose something that you find interesting and summarize its contents for your classmates.

GETTING HELP ON CAMPUS

If you need extra help, guidance, or basic information at any time during the academic year, you can go to a number of places on campus. Student services vary from campus to campus. Check your catalog or campus directory to find out what services are available. All you need to do is make an appointment. Some of the people who can help you and the services they offer are listed below.

- **Students** who have already taken courses and are more familiar with the departments and professors than you are can give you valuable advice about specific courses and professors.
- **Professors** can answer questions about their departments and the courses they teach. Go to see your professors during their office hours.
- If you need help choosing a major, or if you need more information about the requirements of your major, you can see an **academic advisor** or talk to a **faculty member** in that department.
- If you have questions about your visa or any other immigration matter, see the **international student advisor (foreign student advisor).**
- **Career services** or the **placement office** can sometimes help you find a part-time job on campus while you are a student. They can also advise you in identifying and pursuing career goals or graduate studies goals.
- If you need extra help in specific subjects, many colleges and universities offer programs where students can get individual or small-group instruction (**writing centers, math centers, reading centers,** etc.). Many schools offer **tutorial programs.**
- Many schools offer workshops designed to help students relax and cope with their heavy work load. If you feel you need help in these areas, look for **stress reduction** workshops and **test anxiety** workshops.
- Look in your college catalog under **Campus Services, Student Services,** or **Student Affairs** to see what else is available at your school. In addition to meeting your academic needs, schools generally provide information in many nonacademic areas, such as financial aid, recreation, clubs, housing, and travel.

EXERCISE 1.4

Directions: Read the following examples of students' problems. Where should these students go to get help? Each problem might have more than one answer. Your instructor may ask you to work with a partner.

1. Tran has an essay exam in two weeks and is unsure of the correct format for writing essay answers.
2. Pablo wants to major in Anthropology and wants to know what General Education courses are required.
3. Yuko is having problems understanding the material that her professor has just presented in her calculus class.
4. Claus doesn't know what chapters will be covered on the mid-term exam.
5. Claire attended two years of college in France and wants to know if she can transfer any of her credits to the university she is currently attending.
6. Li wants to go to Mexico during Spring Break and wants to be sure he will have no problem returning to the United States.
7. Ana is unsure as to whether she wants to get a job after graduation or go to graduate school.
8. Lars could use some extra money and has heard there might be jobs in the library.
9. Mario has heard that Professor Bean's course is very difficult and that foreign students have trouble understanding his lectures.
10. Helga understands the material in class and studies very hard, but she gets nervous and performs poorly on her exams.

EXERCISE 1.5

Directions: Think of three questions that you would like to ask your academic advisor about the program you are currently in or the one you hope to enter.

1. _____
2. _____
3. _____

Think of three questions you would like to ask your career counselor about the career you intend to pursue.

1. _____
2. _____
3. _____

SETTING GOALS FOR YOURSELF

Why did you decide to go to college? Is it because it is expected of you, or do you really want to be here? Whatever the reason, you are here now, and you undoubtedly want to succeed. Although it is true that your goals may change over time as you learn more and have different experiences, you should have a set of goals from the very start. Think about what they are.

LEARNING STRATEGY

Managing Your Learning: Identifying your goals helps you become a better student.

EXERCISE 1.6

Directions: Think about what you hope to accomplish in the next few years. Answer the following questions. Discuss your answers with your classmates. (Your instructor may ask you to answer some of these questions in writing.)

1. Why did you decide to go to college?
2. Why did you choose this school?
3. What would you like to **major** in?
4. Why does this major interest you?
5. Is there a subject you would rather major in, but you feel that it is not practical? Explain.
6. What **grade point average (GPA)** do you expect to maintain during your first year in college?
7. What **degree** do you hope to get?
8. What do you hope to do when you graduate from college? Why does this interest you?
9. Do you feel confident that you will reach your goals, or do you have doubts? Are your goals realistic?

NOTE: Colleges and universities have academic advisers and career counseling centers. You can find out more about these services in your college catalog. If you need to talk to someone about your goals, go to the appropriate office.

LEARNING STRATEGY

Managing Your Learning: Discussing your goals with experts helps you to make important decisions.

EXERCISE 1.7

Directions: Write about or discuss the following questions.

Think about the type of personality that you have. What personality traits do you have that will help you reach your goals? What personality traits will hinder you?

DEVELOPING GOOD STUDY HABITS

After you consider your goals, it's important to take a close look at your study habits. You have to have good work habits from the first day of the semester. It's too late to change your habits at mid-term. Too much valuable time will have been lost by then.

EXERCISE 1.8

Directions: Answer these questions about yourself. Be honest. Circle the correct response.

1. Are you organized?
   a. never
   b. rarely
   c. sometimes
   d. usually
   e. always
2. Do you procrastinate?
   a. always
   b. often
   c. sometimes
   d. rarely
   e. never
3. Do you enjoy school?
   a. no
   b. on rare occasions
   c. occasionally
   d. often
   e. yes
4. Were you a good student in high school?
   a. F student
   b. D student
   c. C student
   d. B student
   e. A student
5. Do you actively participate in your classes?
   a. never
   b. rarely
   c. sometimes
   d. often
   e. always

6. Do you have trouble concentrating?
   a. almost always
   b. usually
   c. sometimes
   d. rarely
   e. almost never

7. Do you avoid tasks that you don't enjoy?
   a. yes
   b. usually
   c. sometimes
   d. seldom
   e. no

8. Do you avoid work when you feel bored or tired?
   a. yes
   b. often
   c. sometimes
   d. rarely
   e. no

9. If you aren't doing well in a class, do you blame the instructor?
   a. almost all of the time
   b. usually
   c. sometimes
   d. rarely
   e. almost never

Compare your answers with your classmates' responses. Try to evaluate your work habits and your attitude. What areas do you need to improve? As difficult as it may be, you might have to make some serious changes in your approach to academic work.

LEARNING STRATEGY

Managing Your Learning: Evaluating your study habits and changing them if necessary helps you to be successful.

EXERCISE 1.9

Directions: Write about or discuss the following questions.

Do you think your study habits are good or bad? Explain your answer. What steps can you take to improve your study habits?

Now that you've had a chance to think about your goals and to analyze some of your study habits, it's time to start planning your course load.

USING A COLLEGE CATALOG

College catalogs contain very useful information about admission policies and procedures, departments and faculty members, campus services, course requirements, and much more. These catalogs can be purchased in the bookstore on campus, or they can be sent to you by mail.

The library should have copies of catalogs from many colleges and universities. Ask a librarian where the college catalogs are located. If the library doesn't have the catalog you need, call or write to the university for a copy.

NOTE: College catalogs in libraries are often out-of-date. Be sure to check the date on the catalog you are using. If it is not a current one, you will have to call the university to get up-to-date application deadlines and other important information.

The following exercises contain information taken from college catalogs. Practice reading and interpreting the valuable information found in these catalogs.

EXERCISE 1.10

Directions: All catalogs contain an academic calendar. Study this one and answer the questions that follow. Your instructor may ask you to work with a partner.

Threads

In 1821, Emma Willard founded Troy Female Seminary, the first women's college in the United States.

The World Almanac and Book of Facts, 1994

ACADEMIC CALENDAR

FALL SEMESTER:

August 23	Fall semester begins
August 26	Instruction begins
September 6	Labor Day (campus closed)
November 26–27	Thanksgiving Holiday (campus closed)
December 13	Last day of classes
December 14–17	Final exams
December 20	Winter recess begins

SPRING SEMESTER:

January 1	New Year's Day (campus closed)
January 17	Martin Luther King, Jr.'s Birthday (campus closed)
January 22	Spring semester begins
January 24	Instruction begins
March 28–April 2	Spring recess
April 4	Classes resume
May 13	Last day of classes
May 16–19	Final exams
May 21	Commencement
May 30	Memorial Day (campus closed)

---

1. Colleges and universities divide the academic year into **semesters, trimesters,** or **quarters.** What system does this university have?
2. When do classes start in the fall? In the spring?
3. When do classes start after spring break?
4. When do classes end in the fall? In the spring?
5. When is graduation?
6. Can you use the library during winter recess? On New Year's Day? During spring recess?

EXERCISE 1.11

Directions: Catalogs also have detailed calendars with admission information and enrollment deadlines. Look at this calendar and answer the questions that follow. Your instructor may ask you to work with a partner.

NOTE: The calender below gives information for **undergraduate** students. If you are a **graduate** student, the catalog will likely have separate sections with graduate information. Be sure to look at the correct information.

UNDERGRADUATE ADMISSION AND ENROLLMENT INFORMATION

	FALL QUARTER 1994	WINTER QUARTER 1995	SPRING QUARTER 1995
ADMISSION			
Opening date to file application	Nov. 1, '93	July 1, '94	Oct. 1, '94
Deadline for financial aid application	Mar. 2, '94	Nov. 1, '94	Feb. 1, '95
Open enrollment	Aug. 1–Sept. 20	Dec. 9–30	Mar. 16–24
Deadline to enroll without late fee	Sept. 21	Dec. 30	Mar. 24
QUARTER BEGINS	Sept. 18	Jan. 3	Mar. 27
Late registration for all students	Sept. 26–Oct. 11	Jan. 6-17	Mar. 30–Apr. 10
INSTRUCTION BEGINS	Sept. 26	Jan. 6	Mar. 30
Add/Drop period	Sept. 26–Oct. 11	Jan. 6-17	Mar. 30–Apr. 10
Deadline to pay registration fees	Oct. 11	Jan. 17	Apr. 10
Final day to add courses	Oct. 11	Jan. 17	Apr. 10
Last day to change grading option	Oct. 25	Jan. 31	Apr. 24
Last day to withdraw without a "W"	Oct. 25	Jan. 31	Apr. 24
Last day to drop with a "W"	Dec. 2	Mar. 6	May 29
INSTRUCTION ENDS	Dec. 5	Mar. 13	June 5
Final exams	Dec. 9–14	Mar. 16–21	June 8–13
Final day to request grade of "incomplete"	Dec. 13	Mar. 20	June 12
QUARTER ENDS	Dec. 14	Mar. 21	June 13
Commencement			June 14
Grades mailed	Jan. 3	Apr. 8	July 6

1. What type of session does this university have?
2. Approximately how long is each session?
3. If you want to begin studying in Spring 1995, when should you begin the application process?
4. What are the dates of the **drop/add** period in the winter session?
5. When is the last day you can opt to take a **pass/fail** grade rather than a letter grade in the fall session?

6. What will appear on your grade report if you **withdraw** from a course on April 12?
7. What will appear on your grade report if you withdraw from a course on April 25?
8. If you are unable to complete all of your course work, will you always get an "F"? Is there another option? What do you have to do?
9. What is the last day of final exams in the spring session?
10. When is graduation?

NOTE: Colleges and universities are very strict about all deadlines. Pay careful attention to them. If you can't find the dates that you need in your catalog, call or go to the appropriate office on campus to get the information.

EXERCISE 1.12

Directions: Catalogs also have descriptions of individual courses offered in all the academic departments. This information will help you decide which courses to take. Try to answer the following questions based on this entry. Your instructor may ask you to work with a partner.

> **ANTH 102. Cultural Anthropology: Introduction   (4)**
> An introduction to the anthropological approach to understanding human behavior, with an examination of data from a selection of societies and cultures.
>
> **ANTH 105. Social Anthropology   (4)**
> A systematic analysis of social anthropology and of the concepts and constructs required for cross-cultural and comparative study of human society. *Prerequisite: ANTH 102 or equivalent.* (Required core course for anthropology major.)

1. These courses are listed in what **department**?
2. What is the course number of the first listing? What is the title of the course? What is the number of **credit hours** given for this course?
3. What is the course number of the second listing? What is the title of the course? What is the number of credit hours given for this course?
4. If you have never taken a course in this department, can you take the first course? Can you take the second one? Explain.
5. In ANTH. 105, what do you think "or equivalent" means?
6. If you are a major in this department, do you have to take both of these courses? Explain.

Threads

In 1833, Oberlin College became the first college in the United States to adopt coeducation. In 1835, it refused to bar students on account of race.

The World Almanac and Book of Facts. 1994

EXERCISE 1.13

Directions: If you don't have your own college catalog, go to the library and look at a general catalog of your college or another school of your choice. Answer the following questions. Use the index of the catalog to help you search for information more efficiently. (If you don't understand some of the vocabulary in the questions, consult the Glossary of University Terminology in Appendix B.)

1. What catalog are you using? What are the dates on the cover of the catalog?
2. If you are an undergraduate student, find the calendars with undergraduate academic and/or admissions information. If you are a graduate student, find the calendars with information for graduate students. Try to answer the following questions. (If you can't find the answers on a calendar, look in the index and try to find it elsewhere in your catalog.)
   a. Is the university on a semester, trimester, or quarter system?
   b. What is the application deadline for the fall session?
   c. When do classes begin in the fall session?
   d. When is the drop/add period in the fall session?
   e. When are final exams in the fall session?
   f. When do classes end in the fall session?
   g. Are there any scheduled holidays during the fall session? If so, what and when are they?
3. Is there a campus map in the catalog? What page is it on?
4. Look under Foreign Students, International Students, or International Applicants. List the requirements that a foreign student must meet before entering the university.
5. Are **General Education** requirements listed for undergraduates? What are they?
6. Answer the following questions about the History Department.
   a. Where is the History Department located on campus?
   b. How many professors are there in the department? How many have **Ph.D**.s?
   c. What degrees do they offer in this department?
   d. Check the undergraduate courses listed in the History Department. Find any American History course that looks interesting and answer the following questions about it.
      • What is the course title and number?
      • How many credit hours are given for the course?
      • Is there a brief description of the course? What is covered in the course?
      • Are there any **prerequisites** for the course?

USING A COMPREHENSIVE CLASS SCHEDULE

Before **registration** begins each session, colleges and universities print a **comprehensive class schedule** of all of the sections of all courses offered during that session. You need to consult this schedule before you register. You should have already decided which courses you want to take based on the descriptions in the catalog and the requirements of your department. Make a note of the abbreviation of the department, the course number, and title of the course. The schedule will show all the time slots in which this course is offered. It will also tell the location of the class and sometimes the name of the professor. (If the professor is not named, the listing will say "Staff.") You'll have to choose the time that fits into your schedule. This is also your chance to try to get classes with professors of your choice. Here is a sample of some Anthropology courses from a comprehensive class schedule:

Footnotes	Department	Course Number	Course Title	Units	Time	Days	Location	Faculty
	ANTH	102	Cultural Anthropology: Intro.	4	8:30–10:20	MW	ACD 310	Jagger
	ANTH	102	Cultural Anthropology: Intro.	4	17:00–18:50	TTH	ACD 407	Staff
	ANTH	102	Cultural Anthropology: Intro.	4	10:30–12:20	MW	SCI 120	Mills
02 08	ANTH	105	Social Anthropology	4	9:30–11:20	MW	ACD 315	Stewart
02 08	ANTH	105	Social Anthropology	4	13:30–15:20	TTH	ACD 312	Staff

NOTE: A column with special information will pertain to each course. (In the schedule above, this is the footnote column.) Look for the explanation of the numbers and letters either at the bottom of each page or on a chart on a separate page of the class schedule. Be sure that you understand this information. In this particular class schedule, the footnotes are explained in this way:

02 = Course has prerequisite(s). Refer to course description in the University Catalog.

08 = Course is required for all majors in this department.

EXERCISE 1.14

Directions: Use the college catalog entry on page 11 and the comprehensive class schedule entry above to answer the following questions.

1. If you have never taken an Anthropology course before, can you take Anthropology 102? How do you know this?
2. Anthropology 105 uses the footnote 02. Refer to the comprehensive class schedule to see what 02 means. Then refer to the college catalog entry. What are the prerequisites for Anthropology 105?
3. You have heard that Professor Mills is very interesting and you would like to take a course from her. What does she teach?
4. You are an Anthropology major and need to take Anthropology 105, which is a required course. You can still fit a Monday/Wednesday morning class into your schedule. Is this class offered at a time that fits into your schedule? At what time is it offered? What room is it in? Who is the professor?

UNDERSTANDING THE COURSE SYLLABUS

During the first week of classes, professors generally distribute a course **syllabus.** The syllabus is a description of the class, including required textbooks, the objectives of the course, the grading policy, and other important information. A syllabus is an agreement between the student and the professor. The professor is telling what will be offered in the class and what is expected from the students. By taking the course, you are agreeing to the terms stated in the syllabus.

If the professor does not hand out a syllabus, detailed information will be given about the course during the first week. It is very important to attend the first sessions. If you cannot attend, make an appointment to meet the professor to get the information. It is essential that you have a clear understanding of what will be offered in the course and what is expected from you during the semester.

Some syllabi are very detailed with assignments and due dates. Others are less detailed. Keep your syllabus for the whole semester. You'll need to refer to it from time to time.

EXERCISE 1.15

Directions: Your instructor will provide you with a syllabus for this course. Go over the syllabus in class and then answer the following questions. Your instructor may ask you to work with a partner. Be sure to ask your instructor for clarification if there is something on the syllabus that you don't understand.

1. Does your instructor have **office hours?** When are they? Where are they? What is the purpose of office hours?
2. What textbooks are required?
3. How will the course be evaluated?
4. What do you think will be the most difficult part of the course for you?
5. How much time do you think you will have to spend preparing and studying for this course?
6. What grade do you think you will get in this course?

EXERCISE 1.16

Directions: Look at the information on the course syllabus. Think about the rest of the semester and what is expected of you. Is there anything about the course that is still unclear to you? Think of at least three questions that you would like to ask your instructor about any aspect of the course. After you think of your questions, consult with your classmates and see if they have similar concerns. Then ask your instructor the questions.

1. _____
2. _____
3. _____

Testing Hypotheses: Ask for clarification to completely understand what is expected of you in your classes.

DROPPING AND ADDING COURSES

If you feel that you cannot meet the requirements that are stated in the course syllabus, you may have the option of dropping the course and choosing a new one. (However, many undergraduate courses are required and cannot be dropped.) Most colleges have a **drop/add** period. As you know, the dates when you can make these changes are in your college catalog. During this period, you can make changes to your schedule with no penalty. In other words, the changes will not appear on your official **transcript.** However, if you drop a course after the drop/add period, you will have a "W" (Withdrew) on your transcript. Check the catalog and make changes in your schedule early enough to avoid a "W."

Be sure that you have chosen courses you can manage. This is the first step toward academic success.

Overcoming Limitations: Sometimes if you feel that you cannot meet the requirements of a course, you may be able to drop it and choose another one.

MANAGING YOUR TIME

You can't always arrange your schedule the way you would like to, but you do have a certain amount of control. Decide when you are the most alert. Are you a morning person, or do you have trouble functioning in the morning? Do you have a part-time job that you have to work around? Do you like to group your classes together and have large blocks of time to study, or do you like to leave blocks of time between your classes and have shorter but more frequent study sessions? These are the kinds of decisions you will have to make. What schedule works best for you?

EXERCISE 1.17

Directions: Write about or discuss the following questions.

How do you prefer to schedule your class time and your study time? When do you feel the most alert? What time of day do you like to attend classes? When do you prefer to study and in what environment? When and how do you review your course material? Compare your preferences with those of your classmates.

EXERCISE 1.18

Directions: Below are two sample schedules. What are the differences between them? Which one looks better to you? Why? Are there any additions or changes that you would make to these schedules?

Sample Schedule #1:

	Monday	Tuesday	Wednesday	Thursday	Friday	Saturday	Sunday
8:00 am		Art. Hist.		Art. Hist.			
9:00	Am. Lit.		Am. Lit.		Am. Lit		
10:00	– – – – –		– – – – –				
11:00		Study		Study			
12:00 pm							
1:00	Ind. N.A.		Ind. N.A.		Ind. N.A.		
2:00	– – – – –	Study	– – – – –	Study	Study		
3:00	Pre. Anth.		Pre. Anth.				
4:00							
5:00							
6:00							
7:00	Study		Study				
8:00							
9:00							
10:00							
11:00							
12:00							

Key: Am. Lit. *Survey of American Literature (4 Credit Hours)*
Art. Hist. *Art History (4 Credit Hours)*
Ind. N.A. *Indians of North America (4 Credit Hours)*
Pre. Anth. *Prehistoric Anthropology (4 Credit Hours)*

Sample Schedule #2:

	Monday	Tuesday	Wednesday	Thursday	Friday	Saturday	Sunday
8:00 am							
9:00	*Review Am. Lit.*	*Review Ind. N.A.*	*Review Am. Lit.*	*Review Ind. N.A.*	*Review Am. Lit*		
10:00	*Am. Lit.*	*Ind. N.A.*	*Am. Lit.*	*Ind. N.A.*	*Am. Lit.* ↓	*Study and Review*	
11:00	- - - ↓	↓	- - - ↓	↓		↓	
12:00 pm						↓	
1:00	*Review Art. Hist.*		*Review Art. Hist.*		*Review Art. Hist.*		
2:00	*Art. Hist.* ↓	*Review Pre. Anth.*	*Art Hist.* ↓	*Review Pre. Anth.*	*Art Hist* ↓		
3:00	- - - ↓	*Pre. Anth.*	- - - ↓	*Pre. Anth.*			
4:00	*Study* ↓	↓	*Study* ↓	↓	*Study*		
5:00					↓		
6:00							
7:00	*Study*	*Study*	*Study*	*Study*			
8:00							*Review all courses*
9:00	↓	↓	↓	↓			↓
10:00							
11:00							
12:00							

Key:

Am. Lit.	*Survey of American Literature (4 Credit Hours)*
Art. Hist.	*Art History (4 Credit Hours)*
Ind. N.A.	*Indians of North America (4 Credit Hours)*
Pre. Anth.	*Prehistoric Anthropology (4 Credit Hours)*

    NOTE: There will be times when you will have to increase your study hours. You will have to be flexible during the semester. Add study hours when necessary, but don't decrease your hours.

EXERCISE 1.19

Directions: Make a schedule for this semester and stick to it for a week or two. Build study time into your schedule. Include at least one hour of study time for each hour spent in the classroom. (Since you will be studying in a second language, you should allow even more study time.) Be sure to schedule in free time for yourself. You'll need to reward yourself for all your hard work. Use this blank schedule form or photocopy it so you will be able to make any changes after you have had time to try it out. After a week or two, make any necessary changes in your schedule.

	Monday	Tuesday	Wednesday	Thursday	Friday	Saturday	Sunday
8:00 am							
9:00							
10:00							
11:00							
12:00 pm							
1:00							
2:00							
3:00							
4:00							
5:00							
6:00							
7:00							
8:00							
9:00							
10:00							
11:00							
12:00							

In addition to managing your time, you have to be organized and keep up with your work in order to achieve academic success.

- Buy a calendar or a date book and keep a very careful record of all of your quizzes, exams, projects, speeches, assignments, group study meetings, and anything else that comes up.
- Have the telephone number of at least one person in each of your classes. If you are absent, you can call your classmate to find out what you missed. Then you won't be unprepared for your next class.
- Talk to your professor about the course during the office hours indicated on the course syllabus. The professor is there during those hours to help students.
- Be organized and keep up-to-date with your work.
- Review your class notes and reading regularly throughout the semester. Don't put your course material aside for several months and then look at it again right before an exam. You'll end up with too much to review in too short a period of time. **Be sure to build review time into your schedule.**

LEARNING STRATEGY

Managing Your Learning: Review all your course material frequently during the semester.

EXERCISE 1.20

Directions: Write about or discuss the following questions.

What are some of the major differences that you have noticed so far between colleges in your country and colleges in the United States?

EXERCISE 1.21

Directions: Write about or discuss the following questions.

What are the areas that you think will be the most difficult for you as a student in an American university? Make a list of them. How do you plan to cope with these difficulties? Remember—avoidance is not an option.

In Chapter 1, the skills in the following chart were discussed and practiced. In order to show the amount of work that a university student is responsible for, the skills have been divided into two groups. The first column shows work that you will have to do **ON YOUR OWN** and the second column indicates what you will do **IN CLASS.** If you want to be successful in college, you have to assume a great amount of personal responsibility. This responsibility has to start before you begin the first day of classes.

ON YOUR OWN	IN CLASS
Taking Responsibility	
Learning Your Way Around	
Getting Help on Campus	
Setting Goals for Yourself	
Developing Good Study Habits	
Using a College Catalog	
Using a Comprehensive Class Schedule	
	Understanding the Course Syllabus
Dropping and Adding Courses	
Managing Your Time	

Using the Library

INTRODUCTION

In this chapter you will:

- learn your way around the university library.
- use the general reference area.
- find books, journal articles, and newspaper articles.
- work in the library.

Students in American universities are expected to do a great deal of independent work in the library.

Discuss the following questions with your classmates.

1. Have you ever used the library at this school? If so, what have you done there?
2. What kinds of sources can be found in the general reference area?
3. What can you find in the library other than books and periodicals?
4. Are university students in your country expected to do much work in the library? Explain.

LEARNING YOUR WAY AROUND THE LIBRARY

Although each university library is different in appearance, most use the same system to organize their collections—the **Library of Congress classification system.** When you learn to use this system, you can go into almost any university library and find the material that you need. If you have problems using the library, there are always librarians available to help you find what you need. Don't hesitate to ask for assistance.

Before you get too busy with your class work, take a couple of hours to learn your way around the library. Libraries usually have a number of brochures describing the facility and the services. Pick them up and read them carefully. Also, most libraries have maps showing the layout of their collections. Get a map and learn your way around. Better yet, many libraries have tours. If your library offers tours, sign up for one as soon as possible.

Directions: The library has its own specialized vocabulary. See how much of it you already know by filling in the correct answer from the list of words below. Your instructor may ask you to work with a partner.

Check the Glossary of Library Terminology in Appendix B if you are unsure of any of the vocabulary used in this chapter.

reference books   stacks
call numbers   journal
librarians   magazine
circulation desk   microform
periodical index   card catalog/computerized catalog
periodical   bound

1. _____ are used to identify and organize all books and periodicals in the library.

2. The _____ is where you check books out of the library, return them, and pay fines for overdue books.

3. A _____ is any publication that comes out regularly. Some examples are newspapers, magazines, and journals.

4. A _____ is a popular publication that comes out weekly, bi-weekly, or monthly.

5. A _____ is a more scholarly, professional publication that comes out regularly.

6. The shelves where library books are kept are called the _____.

7. Dictionaries, encyclopedias, atlases, and almanacs are all examples of _____.

8. When you are searching for newspaper and journal articles about specific subjects, you must look in a _____.

9. _____ can provide you with assistance when you need it.

10. The _____ is the system that lists the entire library collection.

EXERCISE 2.2

Directions: Go to the library and try to answer the following questions. A map of the library will be helpful. Other answers can be found on signs posted throughout the library. If you are unable to answer some of the questions, ask a librarian behind one of the desks in the library.

1. When does the library open and close during the week? On weekends? (The hours should be posted somewhere near the entrance.)
2. Locate the **general reference** area. (You can ask the librarians behind the reference desk questions at any time when you are using the library. They are there to assist you.) Where is the general reference area located?
3. Go into the general reference area. All of the holdings in the library will be cataloged either in a card catalog or in a computerized catalog (an **on-line** catalog). Does your library have a **card catalog** or a computerized system?
4. The books in the general reference area do not **circulate.** That is, they cannot be taken out of the library. These books are used to look up facts quickly. Walk around. What types of books do you see in this area?
5. Go into the area where the circulating books are kept. (Call numbers A–Z.) In some libraries, the students can walk around the book shelves and get the books without assistance from a librarian. These are called **open-stack** libraries. In other libraries, the students cannot enter the stacks; a librarian will get books for you after you have found the information in the catalog. These are called **closed-stack** libraries. Which type is your library?
6. When you want to **check out** a book from the library, you go to the **circulation desk.** Where is the circulation desk located? What type of identification do you need to show when you check out a book from the library? For how long can you check out a book? What is the **fine** per day if your book is **overdue?**
7. Does your library have:

   a media center?
   a map room?
   government publications?
   a reserve book room?
   a pamphlet file?
   interlibrary loan?
   a video collection?
   a current periodicals reading area?
   computers or typewriters for student use?
   cassette players and headphones?
   group study rooms?

Find these areas on your map and then go to each area and have a look around. What floors are these areas located on?

EXERCISE 2.3

Directions: Write about or discuss the following questions.

How do libraries in American universities compare to libraries in your country? Are university students in your country required to do much library work? What has been your library experience?

LEARNING BASIC LIBRARY SKILLS

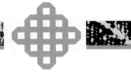

A university library offers many services, but this chapter will focus on the most basic library skills: using the general reference area, finding books, and finding articles in **periodicals** (magazines, journals, and newspapers).

Books are organized on the shelves according to subject. Each book is given a **call number.** Until recently, all libraries used **card catalogs.** These are cabinets with drawers that contain cards arranged alphabetically according to subject, author, and title. Each card contains information about the book and the call number. Call numbers begin with letters A–Z and correspond to the Library of Congress classification system. The call number tells you exactly where the book is located in the **stacks.**

In recent years, many libraries have transferred this information to a computerized system that works in the same way as a card catalog. The card catalog system is basically the same from library to library; however, there is some variation in the software used in the computer programs. Both systems will be discussed in this chapter.

Understanding the Library of Congress System of Classification

Some small, older libraries in the United States still use the **Dewey decimal** classification system. This system uses numbers to divide all books into ten categories.

000–099	General Works
100–199	Philosophy
200–299	Religion
300–399	Social Sciences
400–499	Language
500–599	Pure Science
600–699	Technology
700–799	The Arts
800–899	Literature
900–999	History

The **Library of Congress** classification system, which is used by most colleges and universities, uses a combination of letters and numbers. It divides books into 21 categories:

A	General Works and Polygraphy
B	Philosophy and Religion
C	Auxiliary Sciences of History
D	History and Topography (except America)
E–F	America (History and Geography)
G	Geography and Anthropology
H	Social Sciences and Sociology
J	Political Science
K	Law
L	Education
M	Music
N	Art
P	Language and Literature
Q	Science
R	Medicine
S	Agriculture
T	Technology
U	Military Science
V	Naval Science
Z	Bibliography and Library Science

Threads

The Library of Congress contains over 80 million items in 470 languages.

The World Almanac and Book of Facts, 1994

Books are arranged on the shelves in the library according to these categories. Each book and periodical in the library has its own identification number, or **call number.** The call number appears in the card catalog or in the computerized catalog and on the spine of the book. All items in the library are organized on the shelves according to call number order. We will talk later about using the call numbers to find books in the stacks.

EXERCISE 2.4

Directions: Refer to the Library of Congress categories on page 26 and decide which area or areas in the library you would have to go to in order to do research on the topics below. **(You do not have to answer these questions. You only need to decide which Library of Congress categories they fall under.)**

1. If you are studying French poetry of the nineteenth century, what category would this be in?
2. Where would you find information about the Civil War?
3. If you were studying comparative legal systems throughout the world, where would you look?
4. In what section of the library would you find works on the nineteenth century Utopian movements in the United States?
5. If you were looking for information on prehistoric cave art in southwestern France, in what areas would you most likely find what you need?
6. You are doing research on the drafting of the Constitution of the United States. Where would your books be found?
7. You would like to learn more about the origins of jazz. Where would you look?
8. You have heard that antioxidants can help to prevent heart disease. In what section of the library would information on this subject be found?
9. You have heard that the bilingual education system in Canada is very successful and would like to see how it compares to the American system. Where would you look?
10. What are you planning to **major in** in college? In what area of the library do you expect to spend much of your time?

The 21 categories of the Library of Congress system are broken down into more specific areas with a system of additional letters and numbers. For example, all books with the call number beginning with *P* are on the general subject of Language and Literature. Books will be organized on the shelves in the following order: P → PA → PB → PC →, etc.

P *Language and Literature*

P	Philology and Linguistics
PA	Classical Languages and Literature
PB	Modern European Languages
PC	Romance Languages
PD	Scandinavian Languages
PE	English Language, including Anglo-Saxon and Middle English
PF	Dutch, Flemish, Afrikaans, and German Languages
PG	Slavic Languages and Literatures
PJ	Oriental Languages and Literatures
PK	Indo-Iranian, Indo-Aryan, Iranian, Armenian, Caucasian
PL	Eastern Asia, Oceania, Africa
PM	American Indian and Artificial Languages
PN	Literary History and Collections
PQ	Romance Literatures
PR	English Literature
PS	American Literature
PT	Teutonic Literature

A complete call number will look like this:

PC   PR
64   or   110.3
E6   D53

We'll talk more later about locating books in the stacks by call number.

USING THE GENERAL REFERENCE AREA

The general reference area is the best place to begin your research. This part of the library contains **noncirculating** material; these books cannot be taken out of the library. Dictionaries, encyclopedias, statistical fact books, yearbooks, handbooks, bibliographies, style manuals, and other reference sources are found in this area. The reference area also contains indexes where you can search for magazine, journal, and newspaper articles. All reference sources are arranged by call number. The last part of the call number of all books found in this area will be "**Ref.**" This tells you two things: this book is found in the reference area, and it cannot be checked out of the library.

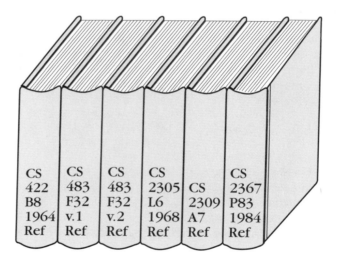

Reference material can be found both in the card catalog and in the computerized catalog. (We will discuss using these catalogs later.) Also, a reference librarian will be on duty in this area at all times. Tell the reference librarian what you are looking for, and you will be directed to the right place. Don't waste your time if you don't know where to go for information.

Using Different Reference Sources

The following is a list of some of the material available in most general reference areas. University libraries generally have very good collections of specialized reference material. You should do your work in the reference area quickly and efficiently. That means knowing what's available and where to look for it. Check the catalog for the call numbers of this material or ask a reference librarian for assistance.

Go over this brief list with your instructor. Be sure you understand the kinds of information that can be found in each of these sources.

General Dictionaries
Random House Dictionary of the English Language
Webster's Third New International Dictionary (3rd ed.)
Oxford English Dictionary (OED)

Specialized Dictionaries (Subject Dictionaries)
Dictionary of Behavioral Science
Dictionary of American Politics

General Encyclopedias
Encyclopedia Americana
Encyclopaedia Britannica

Specialized Encyclopedias (Subject Encyclopedias)
McGraw-Hill Encyclopedia of Science and Technology
Encyclopedia of Education

Style Manuals
Publication Manual of the American Psychological Association (3rd ed.)
MLA Handbook for Writers of Research Papers, Theses, and Dissertations

Atlases
Hammond Atlas of the World
National Geographic Atlas of the World

Yearbooks, Almanacs, and Statistical Abstracts
Statistical Abstract of the United States
The World Almanac and Book of Facts

Periodical Indexes
Readers' Guide to Periodical Literature
Social Sciences Index

Newspaper Indexes
New York Times Index
National Newspaper Index

Biographies
Chamber's Biographical Dictionary
Almanac of Famous People

Book Reviews
Book Review Digest
New York Times Book Review Index

30

Managing Your Learning: Knowing what information is available and where to find it helps you to work more efficiently.

EXERCISE 2.5

Directions: Refer to the list of reference sources on page 29. What kind of reference book would you consult to answer the following questions? In some cases, more than one type will provide you with the answer. List them all, but put the *best* source first. **(You don't have to answer these questions. Just write the type of reference book or books you would consult.)**

Threads

Johann Gutenberg (1400?–1468?) invented movable type.

The American Heritage Dictionary

1. Is Lofoten Island, off the west coast of Norway, north or south of the Arctic Circle?
2. Who had the most home runs in the National Baseball League in 1966?
3. Name five of Thomas Alva Edison's most significant inventions. When were they invented?
4. What is the plural form of *dictum?*
5. What is the capital of New Brunswick, Canada?
6. Find a magazine or journal article on *sleep disorders.*
7. What is the etymology (origin and historical development) of the word *disaster?*
8. You have to write a book report for an American Literature course. Do you think you would enjoy reading the book *Elmer Gantry* by Sinclair Lewis?
9. What was the total population of the United States according to the 1990 Census?
10. What is the name of Thomas Jefferson's home in Virginia, and when was it built?
11. How do you punctuate the bibliographic entries in a research paper using APA format?
12. What was the Gross National Product of the United States in 1990?
13. Who was Harriet Tubman?
14. Which is the preferred spelling in the United States—*encyclopedia* or *encyclopaedia?*
15. Where would you begin your search to find an article about a recent news event?

Testing Hypotheses: If you're curious about something, you can often look it up quickly in the general reference area.

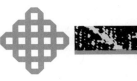

Alphabetizing

Use the card catalog or the computerized catalog to locate books in the library by looking up the subject, author, or title. Card catalogs may be divided into three sections (subject, author, and title) or into two sections (subject and author/title); or they may have only one section with subject, author, and title inter-filed. See how your library organizes its card catalog and be sure to go to the correct section.

To use the card catalog and indexes, you need to know a few simple rules about alphabetizing:

1. **Alphabetizing Titles:**
   a. If a title begins with *A, An,* or *The,* disregard the article and alphabetize according to the second word. Also disregard any foreign language articles. (Articles *within* the title are *not* disregarded, however.)

      EXAMPLES:
      The Grapes of Wrath → The <u>G</u>rapes of Wrath
      The Fall of the House of Usher → The <u>F</u>all of the House of Usher
      Les Misérables → Les <u>M</u>isérables

2. **Alphabetizing People's Names:**
   a. Use a person's last name.

      EXAMPLE:
      John Steinbeck → <u>S</u>teinbeck, John

   b. If two people have the same last name, look at the first name or the first letter that is different.

      EXAMPLES:
      David Herbert Lawrence → Lawrence, <u>D</u>avid Herbert
      Thomas Edward Lawrence → Lawrence, <u>T</u>homas Edward
      James Jones → Jones, J<u>a</u>mes
      John Paul Jones → Jones, J<u>o</u>hn Paul

   c. If the last name is hyphenated, or if the last name has a prefix with a hyphen or an apostrophe, it is considered part of the last name. If the last name has a prefix that is not separated from the rest of the last name with a space, it is considered part of the last name.

      EXAMPLES:
      Nikos Costa-Gavros → <u>C</u>osta-Gavros, Nikos
      Eugene O'Neill → <u>O</u>'Neill, Eugene
      Archibald MacLeish → <u>M</u>acLeish, Archibald

   d. The rules for alphabetizing a last name that has a prefix without a hyphen or an apostrophe, or a last name that has a space separating the prefix from the rest of the last name are very complicated. According to the *Anglo American Cataloguing Rules* (2nd ed.), the rules differ depending on the language of the person. For example, the prefix may be part of the

31

last name if the person is English, but not part of the last name if the person is Dutch. It's not necessary to learn the rules. Sometimes you will have to look up the name in two different places before you find it.

Some names use the prefix as part of the last name:

EXAMPLE:
Daphne Du Maurier → Du Maurier, Daphne

Other names do not use the prefix as part of the last name:

EXAMPLE:
Johann Wolfgang von Goethe → Goethe, Johann Wolfgang von

   e. Asian names usually have the family name in the first position.

EXAMPLE:
Zhang Yimou → Zhang Yimou

   f. Titles of nobility or honor do not change. A title does not change if it doesn't contain a real name. Titles given to performers or notorious characters do not change.

EXAMPLES:
Duchess of York → Duchess of York
Catherine the Great → Catherine the Great
Father Time → Father Time
Buffalo Bill → Buffalo Bill
Mad Max → Mad Max

3. Alphabetizing Subject Headings:
   a. Subject headings are alphabetized according to the following rules:
     • Subject headings without subdivisions come first.
     • Subject headings with subdivisions follow.
     • Subject headings that include any time sequence are filed chronologically.

EXAMPLES:
Architects
Architecture
Architecture, Modern–19th Century
Architecture, Modern–20th Century
Architecture–Queen Anne

EXERCISE 2.6

Directions: Alphabetize the following list of books.

The House of the Seven Gables
McTeague
Orlando
The Return of the Native
Grand Hotel
The Red Badge of Courage
Light in August
Jude the Obscure
Madame Bovary
The House of Atreus
Main Street
The Grapes of Wrath
The Maltese Falcon

Life on the Mississippi
Orpheus and Eurydice
Rebecca
Macbeth
The Red and the Black
The House of Mirth
Remembrance of Things Past

EXERCISE 2.7

Directions: Alphabetize the following list of names.

Charles Spencer Chaplin
Victor Hugo
John Barrymore
Mao Tse-tung
Crazy Horse
Eric the Red
Martin Luther King, Jr.
Georgia O'Keeffe
Lionel Barrymore
Eugene Victor Debs
Vincent van Gogh
Elizabeth Barrett Browning
Langston Hughes
Honoré de Balzac
Cecil B. DeMille
John Brown
Ethel Barrymore
Deng Xiao Ping
Margaret Bourke-White
Phineas Taylor Barnum

EXERCISE 2.8

Directions: Alphabetize the following subject headings.

Americans–Employment Statistics
American
Americana
American Authors
Americans
American Authors–1950s
American Authors–1920s
Americanization
Americans–Living Abroad
America

NOTE: If you are having trouble finding what you are looking for, try looking it up a different way. Perhaps you are using the wrong form of the name. Use the most commonly known name. (For example, use Mark Twain rather than Samuel Clemens.) You might be looking up a name with a prefix the wrong way. Be patient and flexible. If you continue to have trouble, ask a librarian for help.

Using the Library of Congress Subject Headings (LCSH)

If you are looking for information in the library, but you don't know a particular author or title, you can search for material by **subject.** Most university libraries use standard subject headings established by the Library of Congress. When you are locating books by subject, the first step is to look up your subject in the **Library of Congress Subject Headings (LCSH).** This is a set of large red books that gives you a complete list of the headings used in the Library of Congress system. The Library of Congress Subject Headings are located in the general reference area.

Using the LCSH is another way to save time. When you are doing research, you can be sure that you are looking up the correct term. Here is a sample of what you will find in the LCSH.

Eclipses   [QB 175 *(Calculation and Prediction)*]
  BT Astronomy
      Astronomy, Spherical and practical
  RT Occultations
      Transits
  NT Eclipses, Lunar
      Eclipses, Solar
Eclipses, Lunar   [QB 579]
  UF Lunar Eclipses
      Moon–Eclipses
  –1866
Eclipses, Solar   [QB 541-QB 551]
  UF Solar Eclipses
      Sun–Eclipses
  BT Sun

–1854
–Folklore
  UF Eclipses, Solar (in religion, folklore, etc.)
–Religious Aspects
  UF Eclipses, Solar (in religion, folklore, etc.)
  Eclipses, Solar (in religion, folklore, etc.)
  USE-Eclipses, Solar-Folklore
      Eclipses, Solar-Religious Aspects

Key: BT = Broader Term   UF = Use For
             RT = Related Term   –= subject subdivision
             NT = Narrower Term

EXERCISE 2.9

Directions: Answer the following questions about the above LCSH entry.

1. Books on solar eclipses are found under what call numbers?
2. If you look up *solar eclipses* in the LCSH, you will find the following entry referring you to the correct subject heading.

Solar Eclipses . . .
USE *subject headings beginning with the words* Eclipses, Solar

---

UF means "use for." It means that the subject heading "Eclipses, Solar" is used instead of "Solar Eclipses." For what other term in the LCSH would you find the same instructions?

3. If you want to move into a broader area in your research on solar eclipses, what broader terms (BT) could you look up?

4. Look under the narrower terms (NT). These narrower terms are more specific and will allow you to do your research faster and more efficiently. If you wanted to find information on eclipses of the moon, what narrower subject heading would you look under?

5. If you were looking for material on traditional stories and legends about solar eclipses, what subject headings would you use?

Once you have found the correct subject heading, you are ready to search for your book in the card catalog or computerized catalog.

LEARNING STRATEGY

Understanding and Using Emotions: Library research can be time consuming; therefore, be sure to give yourself enough time to do your work to avoid frustration.

Locating Books by Subject, Author, or Title

The card catalog in a library is generally divided into three sections: **SUBJECT, AUTHOR,** and **TITLE.** (Some libraries inter-file two or all three sections.) If you are using a computer, you will be asked if you are looking for **SUBJECT, AUTHOR,** or **TITLE.** Key in **S, A,** or **T** and then type in the information. The computer software may be slightly different from library to library. However, clear instructions will be given on the computer screen, so working in different libraries is not a problem.

If you are using a card catalog, go to the subject section, find the correct drawer, and look up your subject using the subject heading that you found in the LCSH. (Use your alphabetizing skills.) A subject card will look like this:

Subject Card:

QB
175
H69

ECLIPSES

Hoyle, Fred Sir

On Stonehenge / Fred Hoyle
    San Francisco: W. H. Freeman, c1977
    viii, 157 p.:[1] leaf of plates; ill,
    21 cm.
    bibliography and notes

    1. Eclipses. 2. Astronomical Instruments
    3. Stonehenge (England)

EXERCISE 2.10

Directions: Study the subject card on page 35 and try to answer the following questions. Your instructor may ask you to work with a partner. Be sure to ask your instructor for clarification if you are unable to answer any of the questions.

1. What is the title of the book?
2. Who is the author?
3. Who is the publisher of the book? What is the place and year of publication?
4. What does "viii" mean?
5. What does "21 cm" mean? Who needs this information?
6. What is the call number?
7. You looked for this book under the subject heading ECLIPSES. This card would also be found under what other subject headings?
8. What does "ill" mean?
9. How many pages are in this book?
10. There is a **bibliography** in this book. What is a bibliography?

If you look up the author (Hoyle, Fred) in the author section of the card catalog or the title (*On Stonehenge*) in the title section, the cards will look almost the same as the subject card. Compare the three cards.

Author Card:

QB
175
H69

Hoyle, Fred

On Stonehenge / Fred Hoyle
    San Francisco: W. H. Freeman, c1977
    viii, 157 p.:[1] leaf of plates; ill,
    21 cm.
    bibliography and notes

    1. Eclipses. 2. Astronomical Instruments
3. Stonehenge (England)

Title Card:

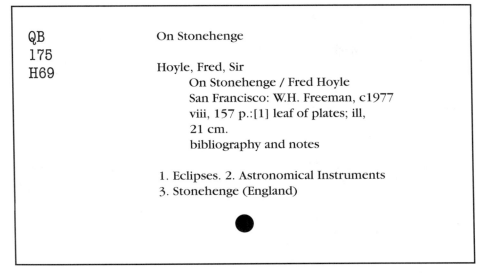

```
QB              On Stonehenge
175
H69             Hoyle, Fred, Sir
                    On Stonehenge / Fred Hoyle
                    San Francisco: W.H. Freeman, c1977
                    viii, 157 p.:[1] leaf of plates; ill,
                    21 cm.
                    bibliography and notes

                1. Eclipses. 2. Astronomical Instruments
                3. Stonehenge (England)
```

If you are using a computerized catalog, follow the simple directions that appear on the screen as you work. As you begin to search for material, the screen will look something like this:

```
You may search for library materials by any of the
following:

        A>      AUTHOR
        T>      TITLE
        W>      Key WORDS in TITLE
        S>      SUBJECT

        C>      CALL #
        M>      ALT. CALL #
        G>      DOCUMENT #

        R>      RESERVE LISTS
        I>      LIBRARY INFORMATION

Choose one (A, T, W, S, C, M, G, R, or I)
```

Choose **S** for **SUBJECT**, **A** for **AUTHOR**, or **T** for **TITLE**. Another screen will appear, and you will type in your information. The next screen will begin to list the library's holdings. You have to start scanning through them until you find what you want. (This is similar to looking through the cards in a card catalog.) Always follow the simple directions at the bottom of the screen.

You searched for the SUBJECT: ECLIPSES
8 subjects found with 34 entries; Subjects 1-8 are:

1. Eclipses → see related subjects .... 3 entries
2. Eclipses .... 23 entries
3. Eclipses chronology .... 1 entry
4. Eclipses early works to 1800 .... 3 entries
5. Eclipses, Lunar.. 1 entry
6. Eclipses Moon Early works to 1800.. 1 entry
7. Eclipses, Solar... 1 entry
8. Eclipses in Religion, Folklore, etc. .... 1 entry

Please type the NUMBER of the item you want to see, OR:

F>	go FORWARD	A>	ANOTHER search by SUBJECT
R>	RETURN to browsing	P>	PRINT
N>	NEW search	O>	Other OPTIONS

Choose one (F, R, N, A, P, or O)

When you find an entry for a particular book, the screen will look like this. Notice that the computer entry for the book *On Stonehenge* looks very similar to the card catalog entry.

You searched for the SUBJECT: ECLIPSES

AUTHOR	Hoyle, Fred, Sir
TITLE	On Stonehenge / Fred Hoyle
PUBLISHER	San Francisco: W. H. Freeman, 1977
DESCRIPTION	viii, 157 p.[1] leaf of plates: ill, 21 cm.
NOTE(S)	Includes bibliographies and notes
SUBJECT(S)	Eclipses
	Astronomical Instruments
	Stonehenge (England)
CALL #	QB 175 .H69

LOCATION	CALL #	STATUS
book stacks	QB 175 .H69	available

R>	RETURN to browsing	A>	ANOTHER search by subject
F>	FORWARD browse	Z>	SHOW items nearby on shelf
B>	BACKWARD browse	S>	SHOW items with the same subject
N>	NEW search	P>	PRINT

EXERCISE 2.11

Directions: Answer the following questions about the computer entry on page 38 for the book *On Stonehenge:*

1. What additional information is available in the computerized system? (Check the subject card on page 35.)
2. If you would like to look for something new, what letter do you key in?
3. If you would like to see what material is in the same area in the stacks, what letter do you key in?

After you find what you are looking for in the catalog, write down the author, title, and the *complete* call number. Don't rely on your memory. Now you are ready to go to the stacks to find your material

Locating Books in the Stacks by Call Number

Books are organized in the stacks according to subject in order of their call numbers. When you find the book that you are looking for write down the *complete* call number including any references to special locations. Some examples are **Ref.** = Reference Area; **Ref. Desk** = Reference Desk; **Spec. Coll.** = Special Collection; **Fol.** = Folio (oversized books). If you are not sure where these locations are, ask a librarian.

The first row of the call number is alphabetical.

EXAMPLE: P → PN → PP → PR

The second row is read numerically.

EXAMPLE: 72 → 76 → 82 → 89

The third row has a decimal point before the number. The numbers become larger. .63 is smaller than .8. Therefore, .S63 comes before .S8.

EXAMPLE: .7 → .73 → .8 → .82

Here is a group of books as they would be organized in the stacks:

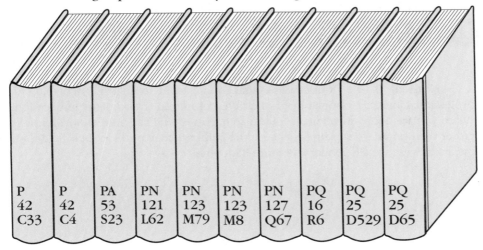

| P 42 C33 | P 42 C4 | PA 53 S23 | PN 121 L62 | PN 123 M79 | PN 123 M8 | PN 127 Q67 | PQ 16 R6 | PQ 25 D529 | PQ 25 D65 |

EXERCISE 2.12

Directions: The following call numbers are mixed up. Put them in the correct order. This practice exercise will help you find books in the stacks later. Check your answers with a partner.

CB 32 B23	CB 31 B2	CB 32 A13	CB 31 B12	CB 31 M81	CB 30 Z23	CB 30.5 N11	CB 513 S11	CA 2006 L13	CB 31 B44

After you have written down the call number, find out the location of the number in the stacks. If the library is large, there will be signs throughout telling which floors the numbers are located on. If the library is small, go directly to the stacks and search for the number. The first two lines of the call number are indicated at both ends of each row of book shelves. The books are arranged in the library according to topic. When you find your book, you will notice that the other books around it are on the same subject. You might want to browse and see if you can find any other useful information.

When you take a book off the shelf, *don't* put it back. You might put it in the wrong place and the next person will be unable to find it. Return the book to a **reshelving area.**

After you have found the books you need, take them to the **circulation desk.** Show the librarian your student identification and **check out** the book. Be sure to return the book by the **due date** or you will have to pay a **fine** for **overdue** books. If you have not finished using the book by the due date, you can bring it back to the circulation desk and **renew** it if no one else has requested it.

EXERCISE 2.13

Directions: List and describe all the steps required to find a book in the library. If your library has a card catalog, describe that system. If your library has a computerized system, describe it. Be sure to use the appropriate library terminology to describe each step.

FINDING JOURNAL ARTICLES

A **periodical** is any publication that comes out regularly: newspapers, professional journals, popular magazines, etc. A **journal** is a scholarly publication. When you are doing university-level research, you should use professional journals rather than popular magazines because the authors are experts in their fields and the articles are usually longer and more in-depth.

To find an article on a specific topic in any type of journal, you have to look in the library indexes. The *Readers' Guide to Periodical Literature* is a general index that lists articles from almost 200 different publications. These indexes come out annually, and the information is organized alphabetically. Here is a SUBJECT entry from the *Readers' Guide to Periodical Literature.* You can also look up information by NAME. (Names and subjects are inter-filed in this index.)

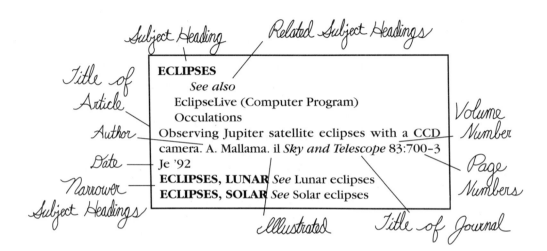

The *Readers' Guide to Periodical Literature* is a general index. Many indexes in the library contain specialized information. For example, some indexes contain only listings of publications in education, business, psychology, and science. Tell the reference librarian what your topic is, and you will be directed to the appropriate index.

After you find what you are looking for in the index, write down all of the essential information: title, author, name of journal, volume, date, and page number. Then check the beginning of the index for the full name of the journal and write this down, too. (Abbreviations are often used in the index entries. You will need the complete name of the journal later on.)

NOTE: Many periodical indexes are now available on **CD-ROM** (compact disks that can each store the equivalent of 1500 floppy disks). Check in your library to see if you can retrieve index information on the computer. If so, follow the directions on the computer screen. The information on the screen will follow the same format as that of the indexes in book form.

EXERCISE 2.14

Directions: Answer the questions about this entry from the *Readers' Guide to Periodical Literature.*

LUNAR ECLIPSES

Comet Swift-Tuttle returns. G.S. Cleere.
Natural History 101:82-3 D '92

December's total eclipse of the moon. A.
MacRobert. il map *Sky and Telescope*
84:670-2 D '92

The moon cruises through the umbra. R.
Shaffer. il *Astronomy* 20:55-6 Je '92

History

Columbus and an eclipse of the moon
[total lunar eclipse of February 29
1504] D.W. Olson. il map *Sky and
Telescope* 84:437-8 O '92

Photographs and Photography

Eclipse photo tips. il *Astronomy* 20:77
D '92

Gallery. il *Sky and Telescope* 84:468-9
O '92

You have to do research on the lunar eclipse that occurred in December 1992, so you look in the index for that year under ECLIPSES. Answer questions 1–5.

1. What is the title of the article which is related to your research topic?
2. Who is the author of the article?
3. What special features appear in the article?
4. What journal is the article found in? What is the volume number? What is the date of the journal?
5. What page does the article begin on?

You read in the newspaper that there will be a lunar eclipse this week and you were wondering if it could be photographed. You decide to see if any articles have been written in this area. Answer questions 6–8.

6. Which article appears to be the most useful? What is the name of it?
7. What is the name of the journal? What is the volume number? What is the date?
8. How long is the article?

You read in a history book that there was a total eclipse of the moon in 1504. Answer questions 9 and 10.

9. What is the name of the article that deals with this topic? Who is the author?
10. What is the name of the journal, the volume number, and the date?

NOTE: When you are searching for information in indexes and you find something that appears to be useful, be sure to write down the complete index entry. You don't want to have to come back later because you forgot one small detail.

Newspapers also have indexes. Some examples are the *New York Times Index* and the *Los Angeles Times Index.* The articles are classified under subject headings. The *New York Times Index* has **abstracts** (summaries) of major news stories and editorials. At the end of each abstract, you will find a notation that looks like this:

Ja 5, B, 28:2
Date Section Page Column

(The Monday–Friday editions of the NYT have 4 sections: A, B, C, and D.)

Ja 7, IV, 31:1
Date Section Page Column

(The week-end editions of the NYT have numbered sections.)

EXERCISE 2.15

Directions: The *Los Angeles Times Index* is set up in a similar way. The entries also indicate if the article is short (S), medium (M), or long (L). Study the following *Los Angeles Times Index* entries and then answer the questions that follow.

ECLIPSES

Thousands of Californians attempted to watch the rare solar event called the "ring of fire" on January 4, 1992, but clouds obscured the view for many; photo. (L) Ja 5 - A, 1:3

A partial eclipse of the moon will block 69% of the moon's surface when it reaches its maximum at 9:57 pm on Jun 14, 1992. (M) Je 13 - A, 21:1

Weather permitting, Southern Californians will be able to see a lunar eclipse on Dec 9 1992, illus. (L) D 9 - A, 3:4

You saw the "ring of fire," and now you would like to learn more about it. Answer questions 1–4.

1. Why were many Californians unable to view the eclipse?
2. What was the date of the eclipse? When did the article appear in the paper?
3. What is the length of the article?
4. Where is the article located in the newspaper?

   You would like to see some illustrations of a lunar eclipse. Answer questions 5 and 6.

5. Is there an illustrated article? What day did it appear in the paper?
6. Where is the article located in the newspaper?

After you find what you are looking for in the indexes, you have to see if your library subscribes to the periodicals you need. A library does not subscribe to all the periodicals in an index. Check the periodical printout in the reference area. This information may be in print form, or it may be on-line. You will need the full name of the journal. (You should have already looked this up in the front of the index.) If your library has the periodical, write down the call number. You should have already written down all of the other necessary information (title of article, author, volume number, date, and page number).

Journals and newspapers can be stored in several different ways: current copies of newspapers and other periodicals are usually loose and are on shelves in a periodical reading room; back issues are usually **bound** or in **microform** (on **microfiche** or **microfilm**). The listing will give you the following information: what form the periodical is in, whether your library has the issue you are looking for, the call number, and where the issue is located. Write down the *complete* call number. Here is an entry from a periodical printout or computer listing.

Title: SKY AND TELESCOPE
Call #   QB .S536

IN SCIENCE CURRENT PERIODICALS:
    UNBOUND ISSUES (QB.S536): kept until bound
IN SCIENCE PERIODICALS STACKS
    BOUND VOLUMES (QB. S536): 1 (1941:Nov)-68 (1984:Oct), 68 (1984:Dec) to latest bound

1> SCIENCE CURRENT PERIODICALS
    Latest received: Sept. 1993 86:3. Last bound: 83-84(1992)

EXERCISE 2.16

Directions: Answer the following questions about the periodical listing.

1. What is the name and call number of the journal shown in this entry?
2. Where are the current issues kept? Why do they eventually leave this area, and where are they later kept?
3. Where are the bound volumes shelved?
4. When did the library begin to collect this journal?
5. What was the most recent volume received by the library? When was the last set bound?

NOTE: One particular periodical can be stored in several ways. The current copies will be loose, but some of the older copies may be bound while others are on microfilm or microfiche. Be sure to get the correct call number for the date you need. Don't assume the entire holding will be stored together. Also, it is possible that certain issues of a publication will be missing. The periodical printout should tell you if this is the case.

Managing Your Learning: Take careful notes and keep your papers organized while you are doing your research to save a lot of time.

EXERCISE 2.17

Directions: List and describe all the steps required to find a newspaper or journal article in the library. If your library has indexes and a periodical printout, describe that system. If your library has a computerized system, describe it. Be sure to use the appropriate library terminology to describe each step.

NOTE: You can't check periodicals out of the library. You can either read the articles in the library or photocopy them. Articles on microform can be photocopied.

WORKING IN THE REFERENCE AREA

EXERCISE 2.18

Directions: Now that you know the kinds of reference sources that are available in your library, try to answer the following questions. To find the call numbers for these reference materials, look in the card catalog or in the computerized catalog under SUBJECT (encyclopedia, atlas, etc.) or under TITLE (*Encyclopedia Americana, Oxford English Dictionary,* etc.). These sources can be found in the general reference area. Refer to page 29 for a list of reference sources. If you have trouble finding anything, ask the librarian at the reference desk for assistance.

1. The word *bluff* has two very different meanings. What are they? (Use any unabridged dictionary. Make a note of your source.)
2. The *Oxford English Dictionary* traces English words from as early as 1060 to the present. Look up the word *college* in the *OED*. What is the year of its first recorded use? Was the meaning of the word the same as its most common usage today? (Use the *Oxford English Dictionary.*)
3. When was the Declaration of Independence formally adopted? (Use any general encyclopedia. Make a note of your source.)
4. What is the name of the largest ice shelf in Antarctica? (Use any atlas. Make a note of your source.)
5. How many cases of AIDS were reported in the United States in 1990? (Use any yearbook, almanac, or statistical abstract. Be sure to use the index. Make a note of your source.)
6. What was the average tuition for a private four-year college in 1980? In 1990? (Use any yearbook, almanac, or statistical abstract. Be sure to use the index. Make a note of your source.)
7. Find a journal or magazine article on *global warming.* (You may be referred to another subject heading in the index.) Since this is a topic which is frequently in the news, you will probably find many articles. Find one which looks interesting and copy the entry. (Use the *Readers' Guide to Periodical Literature.* Then check to see if your library subscribes to that periodical.)

8. Find a newspaper article on *gangs.* Give the name of the newspaper, the date, the section and column, and the name of the writer if it is given. (Use any newspaper index. Make a note of your source. Then check to see if your library has this newspaper in its holdings.)

9. Who was Ned Ludd? When and where did he live? What did he do? Who were the Luddites? (Use any biographical dictionary or encyclopedia. Make a note of your source.)

10. Find a book review on the topic of *feminism* or the *women's movement.* Give the title and author of the book. Where was the book reviewed? (If there are a number of reviews on the same book, choose one.) Give the name of the journal in which the book was reviewed, the name of the reviewer, page numbers, date, and length of review. (Use the *Book Review Digest* or any book review index. Make a note of your source.)

NOTE: Valuable information is given at the beginning of indexes and other reference material in the library. The format is described, and all abbreviations are explained. If you are unsure of how to use these sources, try to find the answer yourself before you ask a librarian.

LEARNING STRATEGY

Personalizing: If you choose your own research topic, you should have some prior knowledge about it or a special interest in it. Have a good reason for choosing a topic.

WORKING IN THE LIBRARY

EXERCISE 2.19

Directions: Choose *one* subject from the first column, *one* author from the second column and *one* title from the third column. Circle your choices. Go to the card catalog or the computerized catalog and find each of your choices. Fill in the form on page 47 based on the information in the catalog. Then go to the stacks and try to find the three books.

Book #1—Subject	Book #2—Author	Book #3—Title
Comets	Virginia Woolf	*Dr. Jekyll and Mr. Hyde*
The Industrial Revolution	Sinclair Lewis	*Of Mice and Men*
	Edgar Allen Poe	*The Maltese Falcon*
Civil Engineering	Charlotte Perkins Gilman	*The Sun Also Rises*
Solar Energy	Emily Brontë	*The Age of Innocence*
Deforestation	Jane Austin	*Sister Carrie*
Computer Technology	Herman Melville	*The Last of the Mohicans*
American Literature	Nathaniel Hawthorne	
The Renaissance		*The Grapes of Wrath*

Book #1: Call Number	Subject: _____ Title: _____ Author: _____ Year of Publication: _____ City of Publication: _____ Did you find the book in the stacks? _____ Yes _____ No
Book #2: Call Number	Author: _____ Title: _____ Year of Publication: _____ City of Publication: _____ Did you find the book in the stacks? _____ Yes _____ No
Book #3: Call Number	Title: _____ Author: _____ Year of Publication: _____ City of Publication: _____ Did you find the book in the stacks? _____ Yes _____ No

EXERCISE 2.20

Directions: Choose a general topic from the list below. Circle your choice.

Feminism	Earthquakes	The Constitution
Photography	Motion Pictures	World War I
Rock Music	Dinosaurs	Cro-Magnon
Acupuncture	Stress	The Rain Forest
The Civil War	Pollution	The Middle Ages

OR

A topic of your choice approved by your instructor

Do some preliminary research to become familiar with your topic. Go to the general reference area and look up your topic in an encyclopedia. Answer the following questions.

1. What encyclopedia did you use?
2. What is the volume number?
3. What are the page numbers of the article?

4. Is the author's name given?
5. Is there a **bibliography** (a list of other books and articles on the same topic) at the end of the article?
6. Does the encyclopedia article provide cross-references or a list of subtopics? (These can be very helpful when you are trying to narrow your topic.)
7. What is the publication date of the encyclopedia? (Look on the back of the title page. Get into the habit of checking the publication dates when you are doing research so you don't use out-of-date material.)

Read the article to get important background information about your topic. Take notes as you read. Write down your source as part of your research notes.

EXERCISE 2.21

Directions: Write about or discuss the following questions.

What topic did you choose? Why does this topic interest you? The topics listed in Exercise 2.20 are very general. Based on your preliminary research, what particular aspect of your topic interests you? Why?

EXERCISE 2.22

Directions: Look up the subject that you chose in Exercise 2.20 in the Library of Congress Subject Headings. In Exercise 2.21, you had the chance to think about the aspect of your topic you found to be the most interesting. See if you can find a narrower term (NT) in the LCSH that reflects this aspect of your topic. Answer the following questions about the listing.

1. What is the general subject heading for your topic used in the LCSH?
2. Did you find a narrower term (NT)? If so, what is it?

EXERCISE 2.23

Directions: From the topic that you chose in Exercise 2.20, find two books. Use the subject heading that you found in Exercise 2.22. Provide the following information about each book. Then try to find the books in the stacks.

Book #1: Call Number	Subject: _____
	Author: _____
	Title: _____
	Year of Publication: _____
	City of Publication: _____
	Did you find the book in the stacks? ____ Yes ____ No

Book #2: Call Number	Subject: _____ Author: _____ Title: _____ Year of Publication: _____ City of Publication: _____ Did you find the book in the stacks? _____ Yes _____ No

EXERCISE 2.24

Directions: Look for one journal article *or* one newspaper article on the same topic. After you have located an article in an index or on-line, write down all of the necessary information. Then go to the periodical printout or the computer and see if your library subscribes to the periodical. If your library does not have the publication, you have to go back and continue your search. If the library has it, write down the complete call number. Be sure to note the form of the article (loose, bound, microfilm, or microfiche.) Provide the following information for the article:

Article: Call Number Form:	Subject: _____ Author: _____ Title of article: _____ Name of Publication: _____ Date of Publication: _____ Volume number (if applicable): _____ Page numbers: _____ Did you find the article? _____ Yes _____ No

NOTE: In the early stages of your research, you may find that your topic was not a good choice. It may be too general or there may not be adequate material on your topic available in the library. At this time, you can either rethink your approach to the topic or, if you are able, choose a new one. It's important to make these decisions very early, before you spend too much time in the library doing research.

Overcoming Limitations: Do some preliminary reading and thinking about a research topic to make sure you can handle the topic before you make a final decision.

NOTE: If your library does not have the books or journals that you need, perhaps you can find them in another library. Check with the **Interlibrary Loan** office and see if you can find what you need elsewhere. If you borrow material from another library, it usually takes at least two weeks to receive it. It's necessary to plan ahead.

EXERCISE 2.25

Directions: Write about or discuss the following questions.

Your instructor may ask you to prepare a brief oral or written report on the topic which you chose in Exercise 2.20. Detailed instructions will be given to you by your instructor.

EXERCISE 2.26

Directions: Discuss the following questions.

Do you feel comfortable and confident using the library now? Is there anything that you still find difficult or confusing?

CAUTION: All libraries are equipped with security systems. Each book has a magnetic strip inside that needs to be deactivated at the circulation desk before you remove it from the library. If you take any material out of the library without properly checking it out, an alarm will go off.

In Chapter 2, the following skills were discussed and practiced. Your library work will be done entirely **ON YOUR OWN.**

ON YOUR OWN	IN CLASS
Learning Your Way Around the Library	
Learning Basic Library Skills	
Understanding the Library of Congress System of Classification	
Using the General Reference Area	
Using Different Reference Sources	
Finding Books	
Alphabetizing	
Using the Library of Congress Subject Headings	
Locating Books by Subject, Author, or Title	
Finding Books in the Stacks	
Finding Journal Articles	
Finding Newspaper Articles	
Locating Periodicals in the Library	
Working in the General Reference Area	
Working in the Library	

Reading, Notetaking, and Taking an Objective Test

3

CHAPTER

In this chapter you will:

- organize your course material.
- read and underline your textbook assignments.
- study as you read.
- practice taking lecture notes.
- practice paraphrasing.
- prepare for and take an objective test.

In college, it's not unusual to have only two tests during the entire semester—a **mid-term exam** and a **final exam.** If you wait until right before one of these major exams to start to review several months of material, you'll be overwhelmed with the amount of work that you have to do. Keep up with your work. Review your notes and reading frequently throughout the semester.

Discuss the following questions with your classmates.

1. Do you have trouble getting through all of your textbook reading?
2. After you finish reading, can you remember what you read? What techniques do you use to help you remember?
3. Are you able to take adequate notes while you are listening to a lecture? Explain.
4. Do you begin to study for a test well in advance, or do you like to **cram** right before a test? Explain.
5. How do you organize your course notes and handouts?
6. Do you have trouble keeping up with your work and **deadlines**? What are the consequences of turning in your work late?
7. When you do academic research in your country, what are the rules for citing another person's words? What are the rules in the United States?

ORGANIZING YOUR COURSE MATERIAL

As we discussed in Chapter 1, it's important to attend all your classes and to keep up with your work. Make a schedule and stick to it. Get to know your professors, your classmates, and your advisor. Take advantage of your professors' office hours.

It's also important to take care of yourself physically. Eat properly, get enough sleep, and try to exercise regularly. If you stay in good physical condition, you'll be mentally alert, have better concentration, and be much more energetic. This may be difficult to achieve, but it can make a big difference in your academic performance.

Try to be organized. We already looked at time management, the way you organize your time. Now look at the way you organize your course material. Have a separate spiral notebook or a separate section in a loose-leaf notebook for each of your courses. Organize your syllabus, handouts, assignments, and quizzes for each course. Keep all of this with your lecture notes for the course. This material will be useful when it is time to study for an exam or prepare a project.

The next step toward achieving academic success is mastering the skills of reading, listening, writing, and test-taking. You have probably spent many years studying these skills in your English language classes, but the focus was probably on interpersonal communication. Now, the approach will be different. In this chapter, we will work on study-reading techniques, taking notes while listening to academic lectures, and taking objective tests.

LEARNING STRATEGY

Managing Your Learning: Improving your study habits helps you to be successful in college.

NOTE: All excerpts in this chapter have been taken from "Culture: Our Invisible Teacher," in *Communication Between Cultures,* by Larry A. Samovar and Richard E. Porter. (Copyright © 1991 by Wadsworth, Inc. Reprinted by permission.) The complete chapter begins on page 134. Before starting to work with this material, consider the following questions.

EXERCISE 3.1

Directions: Write about or discuss the following questions.

How do you define the word *culture*? Be as specific as you can in your definition. Has it been easy or difficult to adapt to American culture? What cultural similarities have you noticed since coming to the United States? What differences have you noticed? Explain your answer.

LEARNING STRATEGY

Managing Your Learning: Identifying what you already know about a subject improves your understanding of the new material.

University students are often surprised by the amount of reading that is required. Reading will probably take a good deal of your time, leaving you less time to study. The solution is to study as you read. After some basic preparation, we will discuss the SQ3R reading method, a very successful study/reading system.

Recognizing the Topic, Main Idea, and Details in a Paragraph

Before you start to read whole textbook chapters, look at the four parts of a paragraph. Each paragraph has: (1) a **topic** (or **subject**), (2) a **main idea** (or **topic sentence**), (3) **key details,** and (4) **less important details.**

Recognizing these parts of a paragraph will help you know what to underline when you are reading your textbooks. It will also help you distinguish between important points and less important points when you are taking lecture notes.

To identify the four parts of a paragraph, consider these points:

1. The **topic** is what the entire paragraph is about. It can usually be expressed in a single word or in a short phrase. Every sentence in the paragraph relates to this topic. In Exercise 2.20 on page 47, you had a number of topics to choose from: Feminism, Photography, Rock Music, etc. A topic is very general.
2. The **main idea** is a general statement the author makes about the topic. The main idea will be expressed in a clause or in a complete sentence. Everything else in the paragraph will give the reader additional information about the main idea. The main idea can be found anywhere in the paragraph, but in academic writing it is usually near the beginning.
3. **Key details** give additional information about the main idea. They are more specific than the main idea. Details may take the form of examples, reasons, comparisons, steps in a process, and so on.
4. **Less important details** give additional information about the key details.

EXERCISE 3.2

Directions: To identify the four parts of a paragraph, read the following paragraph and answer the questions.

Although the "carriers" of culture are nearly the same for all of us (parents, peers, church, and so on), the messages they transmit reflect the character of each culture. A case in point is the popular folktale "Cinderella." Although nearly every culture has a version, each culture uses the tale to emphasize a value that is important to that particular culture. For example, the North American version stresses Cinderella's attractiveness as a reflection of her inner qualities. She is also, however, rather passive and weak. In the Algonquin Indian tale the virtues of truthfulness and intellectual honesty are the basis for the Cinderella character. The Japanese story accents the value of intellectual ability and gentleness. In one version there are only two sisters who wish to go to the Kabuki theater. In place of the famous "slipper test" is the challenge of having to compose a song extemporaneously. One sister manages only a simple unimaginative song, which she sings in a loud voice. But Cinderella composes a song that has both meter and metaphor, and she sings it in soft tones. She, of course, is shown to deserve the rewards of such actions. This rather long example shows that the lessons of culture may travel by similar channels—in this case folktales—but they contain different patterns and values.

Source: *Communication Between Cultures,* by Larry A. Samovar and Richard E. Porter; Chapter 3, "Culture: Our Invisible Teacher" (p. 57)

1. What is the whole paragraph about? Give a word or phrase. That is the topic.
2. What does the author want the readers to know about the topic? It will be stated in a clause or a sentence. That is the main idea or topic sentence.
3. Where is the main idea in the paragraph? Is the main idea restated anywhere in the paragraph?
4. How does the author support the main idea? What are the most important points made in support of it? These are the key details.
5. How does the author support the key details? These are the less important details.

Recognizing Signal Words

Specific vocabulary is used to help the reader follow the author's train of thought. The reader needs to recognize these **signal words** in order to understand how the author has organized the ideas in a text. These writing patterns are seldom used alone. There is usually a dominant pattern with other subordinate patterns mixed in. Your reading comprehension will improve if you understand the organization of what you are reading. Your listening and notetaking skills will also improve when you listen for the same signals. Here are some of the signal words used to show different patterns of organization that you need to recognize. Add others as you go through this list.

To emphasize important points:
the key factor   *above all*
most important   *particularly*

To add information:
first, second, etc.   *in addition*
too, also   *moreover*

To generalize:
in general   *generally*
on the whole   *on average*

To give examples:
for example   *for instance*
to illustrate   *such as*

To offer proof:
based on data   *as proof*
to substantiate   *to support*

To enumerate (list):
and   *(number) kinds, types, reasons*
the first, second, etc. *there are several groups*

To show opposition:
but   *although*
despite, in spite of   *on the other hand*

To compare:
similar to, similarly   *like, alike, likewise*
just as   *too*

To contrast:
but   *in contrast to*
differs from   *unlike*

To give definitions:
is   *define*
means   *definition*

To classify:
two groups   *several types*
to classify   *organize, arrange*

To show cause and effect:
because   *the result of*
therefore   *consequently*

To show chronology:
time (hour, date, year) *then*
afterwards   *during that time*

To describe a process:
first, second, etc.   *next*
then   *finally*

To show condition:
if, whether   *unless*
providing, provided   *in case*

To refute:
in opposition   *erroneous*
to lack consistency   *in error*

To show results or conclusions:
as a result   *in conclusion*
because of this   *hence*

To summarize or restate an important point:
to summarize   *remember*
to repeat   *in sum*

NOTE: A signal word is not always used to show how the writer or speaker is organizing ideas. The same message may be given without the use of signal words. You need to recognize these patterns even when a signal word is not used.

EXAMPLE:

Americans wear their shoes indoors. *In contrast,* the Japanese remove their shoes before entering the home.

Americans wear their shoes indoors. The Japanese remove their shoes before entering the home.

EXERCISE 3.3

Directions: Read the following sentences from "Culture: Our Invisible Teacher," by Samovar and Porter. Circle *all* the signal words and then tell what the signal words indicate. (Don't worry about understanding the vocabulary and the concepts at this time. Focus on the signal words and on the organizational patterns that they show. You will have the opportunity to read these passages in context later.)

1. "In many ways Hall is correct; culture is everything. And more importantly, at least for the purpose of this book, *culture and communication work in tandem*—they are inseparable."

    _____

2. "As Thomas Fuller wrote two hundred years ago, 'Culture makes all things easy.' Although this view may be slightly overstated, culture does make the transition from the womb to this new life by giving meaning to events, objects, and people in the environment. In this way, culture makes the world a less mysterious place."

    _____

3. "The assumption is that people who share a common culture can usually be counted on to behave 'correctly' and predictably. Hence, culture reduces the chances of surprises by shielding people from the unknown."

    _____

4. "Hoebel and Frost see culture in nearly all human activity. They define culture as an 'integrated system of learned behavior patterns which are characteristic of the members of a society and which are not the result of biological inheritance'."

    _____

5. "The reasoning behind this position is twofold. First, people who claim the liberal orientation believe that culture is transmitted and maintained solely through communication and learning. All scholars of culture begin with this same assumption—that is, that culture is learned. It is the second leg of the argument that best identifies scholars who take a sweeping view. These scholars contend that the act of birth confines each individual to a specific geographic location, a location that exposes people to certain messages while at the same time denying them others. All of these messages, whether they be conveyed through a certain language, religion, food, dress, housing, toys or books are culturally based; therefore, everything that a person experiences is part of his or her culture."

    _____

6. "Whereas money is considered an artifact, the value placed upon it is a concept, but the actual spending and saving of money is behavior."

_____

7. "Although learned on the unconscious level, the significant perceptions, rules, and behaviors are given added strength by the fact that members of any culture receive ongoing reinforcement for those aspects of culture that are deemed most crucial. For example, in North America the importance of being thin is repeated with such regularity that we all take this value for granted. In addition, the messages that are strategic for any culture come from a variety of sources. That is to say, parents, schools, plays, folktales, music, art, church, the media, and peers all repeat those assumptions on which any culture operates."

_____

8. "In the United States, studies conducted on American values show that most of the central values of the 1980s are similar to the values of the last two hundred years. In short, when analyzing the degree of change within a culture, you must always consider what it is that is changing."

_____

9. "Many mass-communication experts believe that this interconnectedness of culture is at the core of the "cultural imperialism" hypothesis. This hypothesis maintains that by broadcasting American programs to Third World countries, for example, we are making them like us. This argument is that if we send programs that glorify material possessions to a culture that stresses spiritual life, we are touching many aspects of their culture. Or put another way, if you interfere with one facet of a culture you alter other facets."

_____

10. "Like culture itself, ethnocentrism is usually learned at the unconscious level, while we are actually learning something else. If, for example, our schools are teaching American history, geography, literature, and government, they are also, without realizing it, teaching ethnocentrism."

_____

LEARNING STRATEGY

Managing Your Learning: Recognizing signal words can improve your reading and listening comprehension.

Reading and Underlining in Your Textbook

Underlining or highlighting your textbook reading assignments is a difficult skill. Most students seem to underline too much rather than too little. Students who use a highlighter may find after reading a textbook chapter that they have page after page of almost solid yellow or pink highlighting. It's very difficult to study from your text when you've marked too much or too little.

To avoid underlining too much in your textbook, follow these guidelines:

1. Underline main ideas.
2. Underline key details.
3. Underline definitions.
4. Do not underline the complete sentence, only the important words and phrases.
5. Do not underline less important details.

EXERCISE 3.4

Directions: Return to Exercise 3.2 on pages 56 and 57 and underline the main idea of the paragraph. Then underline the key details. It is not necessary to underline complete sentences. The whole sentence may not be important. Underline only the important words and phrases.

Making Notations in the Margins

Making notations in the margins will help you study directly from your textbook. You can note the following in the margins:

1. Make a note in the margin to indicate anything that you feel is important and may be covered on a test (*✳*, *important*).

2. Write *Def. of* _____ next to definitions in the text.

3. Write brief definitions of new words that are not defined in the text.

4. Write *Ex. of* _____ in the margin next to examples.

5. Write a brief heading for enumerations and then put numbers in the margins next to each point (*3 reasons for* _____, *1, 2, 3*).

6. Prepare a list of abbreviations and symbols to use in the margin to attract your attention later. (A number have already been mentioned above— *Ex., Def, ✳,* etc.) Here are a few others.

   ? —confusing

   summ. —summary

   exam —possible exam question

   lect., 10/18 —see corresponding lecture notes from (date)

7. Briefly summarize key points from the reading in the margin or on a separate sheet of paper.

EXERCISE 3.5

Directions: Return to Exercise 3.2 on pages 56 and 57 and make appropriate notations in the margins.

LEARNING STRATEGY

Forming Concepts: Understanding the organization of a text improves your reading comprehension.

EXERCISE 3.6

Directions: Read the paragraphs below. Underline and make notations in the margin as you read. Follow the guidelines on page 61.

The Ingredients of Culture

Our review of definitions of culture should have made it clear that culture is composed of many ingredients. It might be helpful to look at some of these ingredients and their subcomponents as a way of understanding the composition of culture.

The ingredients of culture, like the definitions, often seem at variance with one another. Most scholars agree, however, that any descriptions should include the three aspects submitted by Almaney and Alwan, who contend that

> cultures may be classified by three categories of elements: artifacts (which include items ranging from arrowheads to hydrogen bombs, magic charms to antibiotics, torches to electric lights, and chariots to jet planes); concepts (which include such beliefs or value systems as right or wrong, God and man, ethics, and the general meaning of life); and behaviors (which refer to the actual practice of concepts or beliefs).

The authors then provide an excellent example of how these three aspects might be reflected within a culture: "Whereas money is considered an artifact, the value placed upon it is a concept, and the actual spending and saving of money is behavior."

Source: *Communication Between Cultures,* by Larry A. Samovar and Richard E. Porter; Chapter 3, "Culture: Our Invisible Teacher" (p. 52)

USING THE SQ3R METHOD OF READING

When you are reading academic material, you should never just read. You need to prepare yourself before you read, to check for comprehension as you read, and to review the material after you read. The **SQ3R** method of reading will enable you to do all of this. SQ3R stands for **SURVEY, QUESTION, READ, RECITE,** and **REVIEW.** If you follow the steps in this system, you will understand the material better. You will be constantly thinking ahead, quizzing yourself, and reviewing.

You will read more efficiently and remember more. In addition, you should be able to concentrate more easily when you read actively.

Here is how the SQ3R Study Reading System works:

1. **SURVEY:** This step will prepare you for reading. When you survey, you move your eyes quickly over the page, stopping only to read certain parts carefully.
   - Read the title.
   - Read all of the headings and subheadings.
   - Read the introduction.
   - Read all words and phrases throughout the text that are in **boldface print,** *italics,* or underlined.
   - Read the first sentence of each paragraph if the chapter is short or the first paragraph of each section if the chapter is long.
   - Look at any photographs, drawings, graphs, charts, or maps and read the captions beneath them.
   - Read the summary at the end or the last paragraph if there is no summary.
   - Read any study questions at the end (or possibly the beginning) of the chapter.

     This survey should take you only a few minutes. After you finish, you will know how the chapter is organized and what areas the author covers. You will also have seen some of the new vocabulary. This preparation will make it easier for you to read the chapter.

2. **QUESTION:** Change the title, headings, and subheadings into questions. You can also change words and phrases that are underlined, italicized, or boldfaced into questions. The answers to these questions will be very important parts of your reading. It will be easy to find the answers as you read because you will know what you are looking for. If your book provides questions, you should definitely use them to help you as you read.

3. **READ:** Now you are ready to read. You know how the chapter is organized, what topics are covered, and what questions need to be answered. If you have time, you might want to read the chapter through very quickly without underlining. When you are ready, read carefully. Underline or highlight and make notations in the margins as you read. Follow the guidelines that you learned earlier. As you read, try to answer the questions that you asked before you began to read.

4. **RECITE:** After you finish reading each section in your book, stop and try to answer the questions you formed earlier without looking at the book. You can do this orally or in writing. If you cannot answer the questions, look at your book, review the material, and then try again to answer the questions without looking at your book. Try to summarize briefly the ideas stated in the chapter either orally or in writing. By doing this, you are testing yourself as you read.

5. **REVIEW:** After you finish the whole chapter, review it in its entirety. Try again to answer the questions and to summarize the chapter. If you do this in writing, you can use these notes to help you study before an exam. Review your textbook chapters frequently.

Threads

In 1992, there were 420,000 foreign students enrolled in institutions of higher education in the United States.

Statistical Abstract of the United States, 1994

LEARNING STRATEGY

Managing Your Learning: Surveying a chapter prepares you for reading and improves your comprehension.

EXERCISE 3.7

Directions: Use the SQ3R System to read the following short passage, which begins "Culture is a dynamic system . . . " Follow each part of the directions carefully.

1. Survey this brief excerpt by following the guidelines on page 63. Because the passage is so short, it should take about 30 seconds to do this. After you survey, answer the following questions without looking at the text.
   a. What is the passage about?
   b. How is it organized?
   c. What else do you remember about it?
2. Turn the boldface print into questions. Write five questions.

   a. _____

   b. _____

   c. _____

   d. _____

   e. _____

3. Read, underline, and mark the first paragraph.
4. Ask the questions that you formulated in number 2 that pertain to the first paragraph and try to answer them without looking at your book. If you are unable to answer the questions, look at the text again and review the section. Then try to answer the same questions without looking at the text.
5. Repeat number 3 and 4 for the other three paragraphs.
6. Review the whole passage. Ask and answer the questions again. Summarize the passage either orally or in writing.

> **Culture is a dynamic system that changes continuously over time.** This current characteristic is yet another example of how communication and culture are alike. For you will recall that in the last chapter we highlighted that communication was not static, but rather was a dynamic, constantly changing process. We now suggest that cultures are also subject to fluctuations, that they seldom remain constant. As ideas and products evolve within a culture, they can produce change. Although cultures change through several mechanisms, the three most common are invention, diffusion, and calamity.
>
> **Invention** is usually defined as the discovery of new practices, tools, or concepts that most members of the culture eventually accept. In North America the Civil Rights Movement and the invention of the television are two good examples of how ideas and products reshape a culture.
>
> **Diffusion,** or borrowing from another culture, is another way in which change occurs. The assimilation of what is borrowed accelerates as cultures come into direct contact with each other. For example, as

Japan and North America have more commerce, we see Americans assimilating Japanese business practices and the Japanese using American marketing tactics.

Although invention and diffusion are the most common causes of change, there are of course other factors that foster shifts in a culture. The concept of **cultural calamity** illustrates how cultures change. Reflect for a moment on how the calamity of the Vietnam War has brought changes to both Vietnam and the United States. Not only did it create a new generation of refugees, but it also forced us to reevaluate some cultural assumptions concerning global influence and military power.

Source: *Communication Between Cultures,*
by Larry A. Samovar and Richard E. Porter;
Chapter 3, "Culture: Our Invisible Teacher" (p. 59)

LEARNING STRATEGY

Remembering New Material: Asking yourself questions and testing yourself as you read helps you remember more of the new material.

EXERCISE 3.8

Directions: Read "Culture: Our Invisible Teacher," from *Communication Between Cultures,* by Larry A. Samovar and Richard E. Porter. The chapter begins on page 134. Be sure to use the SQ3R system as you read. Underline and make your notations carefully. You will be tested on this chapter at a later date.

EXERCISE 3.9

Directions: Discuss the following questions.

On page 137, Samovar and Porter define culture as *"the deposit of knowledge, experience, beliefs, values, attitudes, meanings, hierarchies, religion, notions of time, roles, spatial relations, concepts of the universe, and material objects and possessions acquired by a group of people in the course of generations through individual and group striving."* With a partner from a different culture, choose three of the areas from this definition. Discuss similarities and differences in your cultures within these three areas. Be ready to report your findings to the class.

Taking lecture notes, like anything else, is a skill that improves with practice. Good class notes are essential. The professor may cover material in the lectures that is not given in your textbook. The professor is also able to give more up-to-date information in the lecture than that in the textbook. Also, the professor will emphasize key points in the lecture.

Try to do reading assignments before the lecture in order to be familiar with the vocabulary and the concepts presented in class. Here are some additional tips to help you take good lecture notes:

Before the lecture:

1. Keep all your notes for the course together and in order.
2. Use $8\frac{1}{2}$" × 11" paper.
3. Always date your notes.
4. Make a glossary of frequently used terms and corresponding symbols. Here are some examples. Make others of your own. Be consistent when using symbols so that you will understand them later.

ex, e.g.	—example	*exam*	—possible exam question
def.	—definition	*bet.*	—between
w/	—with	↓	—decrease
w/out	—without	↑	—increase
+, &	—and	>	—greater than
✳	—important	<	—less than
imp.	—important	=	—the same as
max.	—maximum	≠	—not the same as
min.	—minimum	$5, 7\frac{1}{2}, 10\%$	—use numbers
etc.	—et cetera	H_2O, NY	—use common abbreviations
?	—confusing	∴	—therefore, thus
∼	—approximately	*text, p. 101*	—see textbook, page ____

During the lecture:

5. Sit near the front of the room.
6. Try to use outline format. Using outline format is a very useful study tool because you can easily visualize the material in your notes that is related and needs to be learned in a meaningful unit. Here is an example:

    I. Main Idea
       A. Key Detail   This material is related.
          1. Example   Learn it in a meaningful
       B. Key Detail   unit.
       C. Key Detail
          1. Example
          2. Example

   II. Main Idea
       A. Key Detail   This material is related.
       B. Key Detail   Learn it in a meaningful
          1. Example   unit.
          2. Example
          3. Example

  III. Main Idea
       A. Key Detail   This material is related.
       B. Key Detail   Learn it in a meaningful
                     unit.

7. Write down only important words—not complete sentences.
8. Use the same techniques you learned for reading to distinguish the topic, main idea, and key details.
9. Use the same techniques you learned for reading to recognize signal words.
10. Write down everything the professor writes on the blackboard. If it goes on the board, it's probably important.
11. Be accurate when writing dates, numbers, quantities, statistics, etc.
12. Listen for repetition. Lecturers will often repeat important points. (Listen for signal words.)
13. Listen for changes in voice. A lecturer may raise or lower his or her voice to attract your attention. This is also a signal of importance.
14. Watch for gestures. They may be used to show importance or add emphasis.
15. Be sure to record any illustrations, definitions, enumerations (lists), results, and conclusions in your notes. (Listen for signal words.)
16. If a professor spends a great deal of time on a certain topic or seems especially enthused about it, write in your notes that this is a possible exam question.
17. Concentrate on the lecture and on your notetaking. Don't let your mind wander.
18. If you miss something during the lecture, leave enough blank space to fill in the information later.
19. Write neatly so that you don't have trouble deciphering your notes later.

After the lecture:

20. If you miss something during the lecture, fill in the information later with the help of a classmate, your textbook, or your professor.
21. Leave a clear margin on the left to add definitions, summaries, diagrams, or additional notes later.
22. If you have time, summarize all or important parts of the lecture.
23. Review right after the lecture. You will retain more information if you review while the lecture is still fresh in your mind.
24. Review past lectures frequently during the semester. Use the study and review sessions that you scheduled on page 18 to do this.

Your class notes should have a format similar to this:

Use the left margin when you review your notes after class to:	Date
• *summarize*	
• *illustrate*	*I. Outline format —Main ideas are written at the margin.*
• *write def.*	*A. Key details are indented*
• *give ex.*	*1. More specific information is indented further*
• *etc.*	*2. Add additional points of more specific information*
	II. Organize your notes
	A. Use outline format
	1. Indent information as it becomes more specific
	B. Leave plenty of space
	1. Fill in missed information later
	C. Use visuals
	1. Include illustrations that the professor gives you
	III. Pay attention to signals of importance
	A. Listen for signal words
	B. Copy what is on the board
	C. Listen for repetition
	D. Listen for change in voice
	E. Watch for gestures
	F. Copy illustrations
	G. Write definitions
	H. Get all points in enumerations
	I. Write down results or conclusions
	J. Summarize the lecture

Managing Your Learning: Make a conscious decision to pay attention in your lecture classes. Plan to concentrate.

IT WORKS!
Learning Strategy:
Reviewing Your
Course Material
Frequently

Students often ask if they should tape their notes and listen to the lecture again in order to fill in the gaps. A full-time student rarely has time to listen to a lecture one or two more times. It's best to take good notes in class and to use your time to study them. Also, attempt to take all of your notes in English. You'll miss information if you try to translate.

If your professor gives you an assignment, a due date, or notice of an upcoming test, be sure to write it down in class. Don't rely on your memory.

EXERCISE 3.10

Directions: Listen to the following brief lecture. Do not take notes at this time. Try to recall the main idea and key details. What key points do you remember?

EXERCISE 3.11

Directions: Listen again and write down key words and phrases. Do not attempt to write complete sentences.

_____

_____

_____

EXERCISE 3.12

Directions: Listen again to the same lecture. This time, take notes in outline format. Main ideas are written at the margin, key details are indented, and more specific information is indented further.

_____

_____

_____

_____

_____

_____

_____

_____

_____

_____

EXERCISE 3.13

Directions: Did you notice any signal words as you listened? What were they?

_____

_____

EXERCISE 3.14

Directions: Listen to the next section of the lecture. Try to take notes in outline format. Do not write complete sentences. Write only key words and phrases.

_____

_____

_____

_____

_____

_____

_____

_____

_____

EXERCISE 3.15

Directions: List the signal words that you heard as you listened.

_____

_____

EXERCISE 3.16

Directions: Listen to the lecture, entitled "Cultural Changes in the United States." Take careful notes on a separate sheet of paper. You will be tested on "Culture: Our Invisible Teacher" and this related lecture at a later time.

EXERCISE 3.17

Directions: Review your lecture notes. Try to answer the questions in as much detail as possible. If you cannot answer them, you are missing some key information in your notes.

1. What is the topic of the lecture? What is the main point that the lecturer makes about the topic?
2. What major events were occurring in the 1960s? How did these events affect and influence the Women's Movement?
3. The Women's Movement had a profound effect on deeply rooted cultural patterns in the United States. What specific areas of change were discussed in the lecture? Describe each one in detail.
4. How did this movement of the 1960s affect American culture in general?

Filling in the Gaps After a Lecture

It's advisable to go over your lecture notes immediately after class. At that time, you can ask a classmate if he or she got specific points that you missed. If your classmate can't help you, look in your textbook. If you still can't complete your notes, see your professor during office hours.

EXERCISE 3.18

Directions: Go over your lecture notes again. If you have any gaps, ask a person sitting near you if he or she got the information. If you can't get the information from a classmate or from the textbook chapter, ask your instructor. Make sure your notes are complete. Then try again to answer the questions in Exercise 3.17.

LEARNING STRATEGY

Overcoming Limitations: Do your course reading before the lecture to be familiar with the new vocabulary and the concepts of the lecture.

EXERCISE 3.19

Directions: Write about or discuss the following question.

Do you think a person who enters another culture as an adult can ever truly adapt to the new culture? Explain your answer.

A **paraphrase** is a restatement of a text using different words. It is often used to clarify the meaning. You can paraphrase key points from your textbook or from your lecture notes. Rewriting the ideas in your own words will help you remember them. You will also have to paraphrase on essay exams and in research papers.

It is extremely important to remember that whenever you cite someone else's words or describe someone else's ideas, you must give credit to the original source. If you don't tell where you got the information, you are **plagiarizing.** This is a very serious offence in American universities. *Always* cite your source. Here is an example:

"Culture enables us to make sense of our surroundings."
(original)

According to Samovar and Porter in *Communication Between Cultures,* culture helps us to understand our environment.
(paraphrase)

The clause that introduces the source of your citation can be written in any number of ways. Just be sure to give the author and the title. If only part of the identifying information is available, give it. Here are some additional examples of introductory clauses:

In "Culture: Our Invisible Teacher," Larry A. Samovar and Richard E. Porter state / argue / define . . .

In *Communication Between Cultures,* Larry A. Samovar and Richard E. Porter explain / say / contend . . .

When you paraphrase, include all the information in the original excerpt. Leave nothing out. (When you shorten the original text, you are **summarizing.** This will be discussed in Chapter 4.) In addition to using synonyms, you can make a variety of grammatical changes in the sentence. These suggestions will help you do the paraphrasing exercises:

1. Use synonyms.

   EXAMPLE: Understanding other cultures is a *complex* matter.
   Understanding other cultures is a *complicated* matter.

2. Use different word forms (noun → verb, adverb → adjective, etc.). Be sure to make the necessary grammatical changes in the sentence.

   EXAMPLE: Culture is our *teacher.*
   Culture *teaches* us.

3. Change the sentence connectors and signal words (similarly → likewise, because → since, despite → in spite of, etc.) Be sure to make any necessary grammatical changes.

   EXAMPLE: Culture is constantly changing on the surface, *but* the basic principles remain fairly constant.
   Culture is constantly changing on the surface; *however,* the basic principles remain fairly constant.

4. Change active to passive, or vice versa.

   EXAMPLE: Culture *is learned.*
   People *learn* about their culture.

5. Change negative to affirmative, or vice versa

   EXAMPLE: *Not one* part of our existence is *unaffected* by culture.
   Every part of our existence is *affected* by culture.

6. Do not include your opinion or additional information as part of the paraphrase.

7. Do not attempt to change vocabulary in the areas of technology (*computer, microchip*), science (*calcium, test tube*), government (*congress, electoral college*), education (*grade-point average, doctorate*), fields of study (*Anthropology, Linguistics*), geography (*Europe, mountain*), language (*noun, sentence*), peoples (*Indians, South Americans*), brand names (*Macintosh, Honda*), or for everyday words that have no synonyms (*dictionary, vitamins, culture*).

8. Do not use quotation marks.

9. Cite your source as completely as you can (author + title).

10. You do not need to give credit to a source if the information is common knowledge. That is, if you heard something on the evening news that was broadcast across the country and was in all the newspapers, you don't have to cite where you heard about this major event. However, you do have to cite specific details and statements associated with this event.

11. Be careful if you are using a bilingual dictionary when you summarize and paraphrase. Synonyms are often slightly different in meaning, and the new word may not work as a substitute for the original word. For example, *The American Heritage Dictionary of the English Language* lists *change, alter, vary, modify, transform, convert,* and *transmute* as synonyms and then defines each one separately and differently. A bilingual dictionary may not give you this information. Use a good dictionary.

    EXAMPLE: The Women's Movement *changed* American culture.
    The Women's Movement *transmuted* American culture.
    (incorrect synonym)

12. Make sure that your paraphrase has the same meaning as the original.

EXERCISE 3.20

Directions: Look at the quotation and the paraphrase below. Refer to the paraphrasing guidelines on pages 72–73 and list all the changes that were made in this paraphrase. Notice that more is involved in paraphrasing than using synonyms. Your instructor may ask you to work with a partner.

"Children, regardless of the culture, quickly learn to behave in a manner that is acceptable to adults. Conversely, they are also told that if they are good they will be rewarded." (original, p. 136.)

In "Culture: Our Invisible Teacher," Samovar and Porter remind us that all children soon learn to act in a way that adults accept. On the other hand, people tell children they'll get a reward if they behave well. (paraphrase)

_____

_____

_____

_____

_____

EXERCISE 3.21

Directions: Look at the sentences below. Find appropriate synonyms (words or phrases) for the underlined words and phrases. Use a good dictionary to complete all the paraphrasing exercises. If you don't have one, do Exercises 3.21–3.24 in the library. Before you go over this exercise with your instructor, compare your answers with a classmate. See if you both agree that appropriate synonyms have been chosen.

1. "Our entire <u>repertory</u> of communicative behaviors depends largely on the cultures in which we have <u>been raised</u>."

   repertory: _____

   be raised: _____

2. "We have already indicated, however, that culture, like communication, is <u>ubiquitous</u>, <u>multidimensional</u>, <u>complex</u>, and <u>all-pervasive</u>."

   ubiquitous: _____

   multidimensional: _____

   complex: _____

   all-pervasive: _____

3. "Culture is not <u>innate</u>; it is learned."

   innate: _____

4. "The <u>various</u> <u>facets</u> of culture are <u>interrelated</u>."

   various: _____

   facets: _____

   interrelated: _____

EXERCISE 3.22

Directions: Replace the underlined words with different forms of the same words (noun → verb, adjective → adverb, etc.). Then rewrite the sentence so that the new word form fits. Make sure that your sentences are correct in both meaning and grammar. These sentences will only be partially paraphrased at this point.

1. "If culture were a single thing we would need only one <u>definition</u>."

   _____

   _____

2. "Within each culture, therefore, there is no need to expend energy deciding what each event <u>means</u> or how to <u>respond</u> to it."

   _____

   _____

3. "The assumption is that people who share a common culture can usually be counted on to <u>behave 'correctly' and predictably</u>."

   _____

   _____

4. "We are now ready to focus on those aspects of culture that one must understand in order to <u>communicate successfully</u> with someone from a different background."

   _____

   _____

EXERCISE 3.23

Directions: Paraphrase the following sentences. In addition to using synonyms or different word forms, try to make some of the grammatical changes given on page 73. Don't leave any information out.

1. "All scholars of culture begin with the same assumption—that is, that culture is learned."

   _____

   _____

2. "Cole and Scribner offer a definition of culture that ties culture to human cognition."

   _____

   _____

3. "The lack of agreement on any one definition of culture led anthropologists Kroeber and Kluckhohn to review some five hundred definitions, phrasings, and uses of the concept."

_____

_____

4. "It is the most difficult to explain because we must ask the word *learned* to stand for more than one thing."

_____

_____

EXERCISE 3.24

IT WORKS!
Learning Strategy:
Rephrasing
New Material

Directions: Paraphrase the following short paragraph on a separate sheet of paper. Be sure to cite your source. Remember: when you paraphrase, you leave nothing out. Your paraphrase should be about the same length as the original. Make sure that the meaning of the passage does not change.

In the United States, studies conducted on American values show that most of the central values of the 1980s are similar to the values of the last two hundred years. In short, when analyzing the degree of change within a culture, you must always consider what it is that is changing. Don't be fooled because downtown Tokyo looks much like Paris or New York. Most of what we call culture is below the surface.

Source: *Communication Between Cultures*, by Larry A. Samovar and Richard E. Porter; Chapter 3, "Culture: Our Invisible Teacher" (p. 60)

EXERCISE 3.25

Directions: Write about or discuss the following question.

On page 144, Samovar and Porter use the example of the Women's Movement in the United States as a cultural change that had a tremendous effect on American culture in general. This was later discussed in greater detail in the lecture. Can you think of a similar example in your country when major changes were brought about in many areas due to changes in a single area?

Studying Your Notes

It's important to review your notes soon after class while the lecture is still fresh in your mind and to review them frequently throughout the semester. To help you study your notes, you can also:

1. With the help of a classmate, your textbook, or the professor, try to fill in any areas that you had to leave blank during the lecture.
2. Paraphrase key points from the lecture. Writing the information in your own words will help you remember it.
3. Add definitions in the margins for any vocabulary that is new to you.
4. Turn headings into questions and see if you can answer them without looking at your notes. (This is the same technique as the SQ3R method.)

EXERCISE 3.26

Directions: Turn at least five of the headings from your lecture notes into questions. Then see if you can answer these questions without looking at your notes.

1. _____

2. _____

3. _____

4. _____

5. _____

EXERCISE 3.27

Directions: Paraphrase the sections of your lecture notes related to the questions asked in Exercise 3.26. Use these notes to help you study for the chapter test.

PREPARING FOR AN OBJECTIVE TEST

The terms **quiz, test,** and **exam** usually refer to the length and value of a test. A quiz is usually very short, possibly as short as five or ten minutes. Each one will count very little toward your final grade; however, if a professor gives many quizzes, the point value toward your grade could be significant. A **snap-quiz** or a **pop-quiz** is a surprise test; it is not announced in advance by the professor. Tests are usually longer than quizzes. Exams are major tests that will count significantly toward your final grade. Some professors give only one or two exams during the entire semester. The syllabus for the course should indicate how the final grade for the course will be determined.

Tests are generally **closed-book** tests. On occasion, a professor will allow students to use their textbooks or other course material during a test. This is an **open-book** test. Professors will sometimes give **take-home** exams. These are done outside the classroom and must be returned to the professor by a specified time. Take-home exams are, of course, open-book.

The two types of tests you'll be taking in college are **objective tests** (multiple choice, true/false, fill in the blanks, and matching) and **subjective tests** (short answers and essay questions). Objective test answers are either right or wrong; the professor makes no personal judgments about the answers. In fact, these tests are often scored by machines. In subjective tests, answers will be graded by your professor, and a great deal of consideration will go into the scoring of these tests. In this chapter, we will look at different strategies to help you when you take objective tests. Subjective tests will be covered in Chapter 4.

Earlier, we talked about plagiarism as a serious academic offence. Another serious offence is **cheating.** If your professor even suspects that you glanced at another paper, you could get an *F* on the test. Keep your eyes on your own paper. And don't let anyone look at your test. You could get into trouble for this, too.

To study for any test, use the study techniques you've been practicing throughout this chapter.

1. If you don't know what kind of test you are going to have, ask your professor.
2. If you don't know the extent of the material that will be covered on the exam, be sure to ask.
3. Quiz yourself as you review the material. Use the study-reading and note-taking techniques discussed in this chapter.
4. You should review your material throughout the term. Begin a more concentrated study effort at least a week before the exam. Don't **cram** the night before the test.
5. Learn information that the professor stressed and spent a great deal of time on during the semester.
6. Professors will often tell students to study particular segments of the course. It is fairly certain that this material will appear on a test.
7. Always go to review sessions. The material the professor chooses to go over during these sessions will almost certainly appear on the test.
8. Look at the course syllabus or the course outline that was distributed the first week of class. It might include a list of key points.
9. Review all tests, worksheets, and handouts given out during the semester. (You should have all of this information if your course material is organized.)
10. Learn the specialized vocabulary that is associated with each course.
11. Learn all enumerations (lists).
12. Always arrive at your exams a little early. Be prepared with writing material and anything else your professor has instructed you to bring.

More study techniques will be given in Chapter 4.

EXERCISE 3.28

Directions: Go through "Culture: Our Invisible Teacher" and the lecture and make a list of at least ten vocabulary words. (Important vocabulary in your textbook might be in boldface print or italics.) Write a brief definition for each word. Don't look up the definition in the dictionary until you have checked to see if the word is defined in the text. Use this list later to help you study for the chapter test.

1. _____
2. _____
3. _____
4. _____
5. _____
6. _____
7. _____
8. _____
9. _____
10. _____

The best strategy for taking an objective test is to study and to know the material. In particular, learn details rather than broad concepts for this type of test.

However, there will be times when you will be unsure of an answer, and there are some guessing strategies that often work. (Notice that I said "often.") Many of these strategies deal with the use of the language, so you may have to think beyond the course material.

<u>For multiple-choice questions</u>:

1. Read the directions carefully. Most of the time, you will be asked to choose the best answer. At times, you may be asked to choose *all* the correct answers.
2. Eliminate the answers you are sure are wrong.
3. Watch for words which express ideas absolutely such as *all, none, never* and *always.* We can rarely make an absolute statement about anything, so these answers are usually wrong.
4. Read all the answer choices, even if you are certain that the first one is correct. There may be choices such as "all of the above," "none of the above," "a and c," "all except b," and so on.
5. If two answers are similar and you think they are both correct, choose the one that contains more complete information. This is usually the longer answer.
6. If two answers have the same meaning, they will both be wrong if you can only have one correct answer.
7. If two answers state the opposite, one is probably right.
8. If you are having trouble understanding a question and/or the answer choices, use your paraphrasing skills.

<u>For true/false questions</u>:

1. Read the directions carefully. You usually have to mark true (T) or false (F), but sometimes you will be asked to correct the statement if it is false.
2. Watch for words that express ideas absolutely, such as *all, none, never* and *always.* These answers are usually wrong.
3. Be careful of double negatives.
4. If you are having trouble understanding a question, try to paraphrase it.

<u>For fill in the blanks</u>:

1. Read the directions carefully. Do the directions ask you to fill in a *word* or *words*?
2. Look for grammatical clues. See what part of speech is missing from the sentence.
3. Read the entire sentence over after you fill in the blank to be sure it makes sense.

<u>For matching questions</u>:

1. Read both columns before you begin. Count the number in each column to see if there will be extras when you are finished.
2. Do the ones you're sure of first.
3. Cross out the ones you have used so you won't be distracted by them.

Short-answer or definition questions can appear on objective or subjective tests. The length of these answers can vary from a phrase to several paragraphs. Follow the directions on the test.

For all types of objective questions, fill in *all* the answers unless your professor gives you other instructions. Guess if you have to. You might get lucky.

EXERCISE 3.29

Directions: Answer these objective test questions. Be sure to follow the directions. After you finish, go over your answers with a partner. Explain why the answers you did not choose are wrong.

Multiple Choice:

Direction: Circle the correct answer.

1. Culture helps us to
    a. understand our surroundings.
    b. predict the future.
    c. make eye contact with others.
    d. a and c
    e. all of the above
2. Aesthetics includes all except
    a. graphics.
    b. language.
    c. folklore.
    d. music.
    e. drama.
3. Direct eye contact is
    a. always culturally inappropriate.
    b. often appropriate in social situations.
    c. culturally acceptable.
    d. never appropriate in the presence of an elder.
    e. none of the above.

True/False:

Directions: Circle *T* if the answer is true and *F* if the answer is false. If the answer is false, correct it.

4. T / F   Enculturation always takes place through interaction.
5. T / F   Culture is not unchanging.

Fill in the blank:

Directions: Fill in the blank with the correct word.

6. "_____ is usually defined as the discovery of new practices, tools or concepts that most members of the culture eventually accept." (Samovar and Porter)

7. "_____, or borrowing from another culture, is another way in which change occurs." (Samovar and Porter)

Matching:

Directions: Match the major elements of culture to the specific factors related to them according to Terpstra in Samovar and Porter.

8. _____ Religion

9. _____ Social organization

10. _____ Politics

a. kinship, social institutions, authority structures . . .

b. nationalism, imperialism, power . . .

c. sacred objects, philosophical systems, beliefs and norms . . .

d. achievement, work, wealth . . .

Reading Directions and Budgeting Your Time on an Objective Test

Before you begin any test, look the whole test over carefully. Read all the directions and notice the number of questions. Decide how much time you can spend on each section. Budget your time carefully so that you can be sure to finish the test. Give yourself a few minutes at the end to go over the whole test.

EXERCISE 3.30

Directions: Decide how you would budget your time for the following tests. Work with a partner and see if you agree on the best strategy for completing these tests.

Test #1: 50 minutes

25 multiple choice	2 points each	50 points
10 true/false	2 points each	20 points
10 matching questions	2 points each	20 points
5 fill in the blanks	2 points each	10 points
		100 points

How would you budget your time?

_____ minutes to preview the test

_____ minutes to do the multiple choice

_____ minutes to do the true/false

_____ minutes to do the matching

_____ minutes to do the fill in the blanks

_____ minutes to go over your test before handing it in

Total: 50 minutes

Test #2: 90 minutes

25 multiple choice	1 point each	25 points
15 true/false with corrections	2 points each	30 points
10 fill in the blanks	2 points each	20 points
10 matching	1 point each	10 points
3 short answer	5 points each	15 points
		100 points

How would you budget your time?

_____ minutes to preview the test

_____ minutes to do the multiple choice

_____ minutes to do the true/false

_____ minutes to do the fill in the blanks

_____ minutes to do the matching

_____ minutes to do the short answer questions

_____ minutes to go over your test before handing it in

Total: 90 minutes

TAKING AN OBJECTIVE TEST

EXERCISE 3.31

Directions: Study "Culture: Our Invisible Teacher" and the lecture. Your instructor will give you an objective test on this chapter.

EXERCISE 3.32

Directions: Write about or discuss the following questions.

On page 144, Samovar and Porter quote Keesing, who claims, "Ethnocentrism is a universal tendency for any people to put its own culture and society in a central position of priority and worth." Do you agree with Keesing? Do you think people from your country are ethnocentric? Do you think Americans are ethnocentric? Explain your answers.

Threads

It is clear that the welfare of the group and of the entire universe eventually depends on the individual.

Dorothy Lee, *Freedom and Culture*

Directions: Discuss the following questions.

Were you able to complete all of the work presented in this chapter? Do you feel that you were adequately prepared for the test? Of the material presented in this chapter, what do you still find difficult? Are you satisfied with the grade you received on the test? How could you improve your performance the next time?

SUMMARY

In Chapter 3, these skills were discussed and practiced. Once again, a great deal of your work will be done **ON YOUR OWN.** You'll have to manage your time carefully and keep up with your work.

ON YOUR OWN	IN CLASS
Organizing Your Course Material	
Reading Academic Writing	
Recognizing Topic, Main Idea, and Details in a Paragraph	
Recognizing Signal Words	
Reading and Underlining in Your Textbook	
Making Notations in the Margins	
Using the SQ3R Reading Method	
	Taking Lecture Notes
Filling in the Gaps After a Lecture	
Paraphrasing	
Studying Your Notes	
Preparing for Objective Tests	
	Reading Directions and Budgeting Your Time on Objective Tests
	Taking an Objective Test

Reading, Notetaking, and Taking an Essay Test

CHAPTER

In this chapter you will:

- prepare study notes from your reading assignments and from your lecture notes.
- practice summarizing.
- work on improving your memory.
- practice speaking in class.
- prepare for and take an essay test.

In Chapter 3, you worked on some basic study skills. In this chapter, you'll practice the same skills and expand upon them. You'll work on some of the areas that can be the most troubling for foreign students—speaking in class and writing essay exams.

Discuss the following questions with your classmates.

1. Do you find it difficult to get involved in class discussions? Explain your answer.
2. Do you sometimes have trouble studying from your textbook and your lecture notes? If so, why?
3. Would you rather take multiple-choice tests or essay tests? Why?
4. Can you sometimes predict what questions will be asked on your exams? How do you do this?
5. When you are trying to learn something new, what are some of the different techniques you use to help you remember the new material?

NOTE: All excerpts in this chapter have been taken from the chapter entitled "The Communication Process" in *Media/Impact: An Introduction to Mass Media* (2nd ed.), by Shirley Biagi. (Copyright © 1992 by Wadsworth, Inc. Reprinted by permission.) The complete chapter begins on page 148. Before starting to work with this material, consider the following questions.

EXERCISE 4.1

Directions: Discuss the following questions.

Mass communication is any form of communication from one person to a large group of people. What are the different forms of mass communication? Who controls the different areas of mass communication in the United States? In your country?

Keeping Up with Your Work

As your work accumulates throughout the term, you may begin to wonder how you'll remember all the new material. In addition to practicing the study skills that you learned in Chapter 3, we'll look at some techniques to help you learn and remember this new information.

Reading and Preparing Study Notes

In this chapter, you will review the reading and underlining skills that you learned in Chapter 3. In addition, you will work on summarizing and preparing study notes.

EXERCISE 4.2

Directions: Read the chapter entitled "The Communication Process" in *Media/Impact: An Introduction to Mass Media* (2nd ed.), by Shirley Biagi. It begins on page 148. Underline the main ideas and key details and make notations in the margins. Be sure to use the SQ3R method as you read. As in Chapter 3, you will be tested on this chapter later.

NOTE: At the beginning of the semester, professors often distribute reading lists to the students. The books and articles on the list give additional information about the subjects to be covered in the course. The readings on this list will either be **optional** or **required.** If they are optional, you can read the material if you want to. If they are required, you *must* do the reading. Required readings are sometimes held in the **reserve book room** in the library. You should have found the reserve book room during your library tour. Material put on reserve usually cannot be taken out of the library. You can borrow it for a limited amount of time and use it in the library, or you can photocopy it.

Threads

Freedom of the press was recognized in 1735 when John Peter Zenger, editor of the *New York Weekly Journal,* was acquitted on charges of libeling a British governor.

The World Almanac and Book of Facts, 1994

SUMMARIZING

In Chapter 3, you learned to paraphrase. The same techniques are used for **summarizing.** You will recall that in a paraphrase all the information in the original text is included, whereas in a summary only the most important information is included. You will include the main idea and key details and omit the rest. There is no rule as to how long a summary should be compared to the original. Generally, a summary will be from one-quarter to one-half the length of the original text. A summary can be as short as a single sentence, or it can be many pages long. The one-sentence summary will be discussed in Chapter 5.

Since most academic writing involves writing from sources, summaries are often required. You will summarize on essay exams, in all research writing, in oral presentations, and as a means of condensing your reading and lecture notes to help you study.

Review the paraphrasing guidelines on pages 72–73. In addition, to write effective summaries, follow these guidelines:

1. Read the original text several times if necessary. You must have a thorough understanding of the original before you can attempt to summarize it. Look up any words you are unsure of.

2. Underline the main idea and the key details. It is not necessary to underline complete sentences.

3. Write notes in the margin, restating what you underlined. Use your own words.

4. Use the same techniques you practiced in the paraphrasing exercises:
   a. Use synonyms.
   b. Use different word forms.
   c. Use different sentence connectors and signal words.
   d. Change active to passive, or vice versa.
   e. Change negative to affirmative, or vice versa.
   f. Change grammatical structures as necessary.
   g. Do not attempt to change specialized vocabulary.

5. Begin to write your summary. Look at your handwritten notes, not at the underlined parts of the text. This way, you will not be tempted to use the original wording in your summary.

6. Do not use quotation marks.

7. Cite the author and title in the first sentence of your summary. Always cite your source, as you learned to do in Chapter 3.

8. Use the same type of organization as the original text. For example, if the original text shows contrast, be sure that your summary clearly indicates contrast. If the original shows cause and effect, the summary must do the same. If the original gives a number of examples, give a few examples in your summary.

9. If the author's tone or attitude was clear in the original text, show this in your summary. For example, let the reader know if the author was angry, uncertain, insistent, and so on. The verb used in your introductory clause can indicate tone or attitude (e.g., "The author *states / denies / suggests / insists / complains / orders / warns,*" and so on.)

10. Don't include your opinions or any additional information as part of your summary.

11. An author will often repeat important points. Don't repeat in a summary.

12. Make sure your summary has the same meaning as the original.

Study the following paragraph and summary. Notice that the summary was written from the marginal notes and not from the original text.

IT WORKS!
Learning Strategy:
Rephrasing
New Material

People always have an inherent need to communicate. We must be able to store, carry, and have access to information for modern mass communication.

> This <u>effort to communicate</u>—first through spoken messages, then through pictographs, then through the written word, and finally through printed words—<u>demonstrates people's innate desire to share information</u> with one another. *<u>Storability, portability, and accessibility</u>* of information are <u>essential to today's concept of mass communication</u>. (original—45 words)
>
> Source: "The Communication Process" from *Media/Impact: An Introduction to Mass Media* (2nd ed.), by Shirley Biagi (p. 24)

> In *Media/Impact,* Shirley Biagi explains that people have always had an inherent need to communicate. The ability to store, carry, and have access to information is necessary in modern mass communication. (summary—32 words)

EXERCISE 4.3

Directions: Read the original text carefully. Then look at the summary that follows. The summary contains errors that change the meaning of the original text. Find the errors and correct this faulty summary. Your instructor may ask you to work with a partner.

The Greek philosopher Socrates anticipated the changes that widespread literacy would bring. He argued that knowledge should remain among the privileged class. Writing threatened the exclusive use of information, he said: "Once a thing is put in writing, the composition, whatever it may be, drifts all over the place, getting into the hands not only of those who understand it, but equally of those who have no business with it." (original—70 words)

Source: "The Communication Process" from *Media/Impact: An Introduction to Mass Media* (2nd ed.), by Shirley Biagi (p. 23)

Shirley Biagi states in "The Communication Process" that Socrates remarked that extensive communication would take information away from the educated, where he felt it belonged. (summary—25 words)

EXERCISE 4.4

Directions: Read the short paragraphs below. Underline the main idea and the key details. Make notes in the margins using your own words. Then summarize the paragraphs. Be sure to include all the key information. Follow the guidelines on page 88. Compare the number of words in your summary with the number in the original text. Include the author and title for the first summary, but leave the information out for the other four since they all come from the same source.

1. "To understand the mass media, first it is important to understand the process of communication. Communication is the act of sending ideas and attitudes from one person to another. Writing and talking to each other are only two ways human beings communicate. We also communicate when we gesture, move our bodies, or roll our eyes." (p. 149—55 words)

_____

_____

_____

_____

Number of words: _____

2. "What you see, read, and hear in the American mass media may cajole, entertain, inform, persuade, provoke, and even perplex you. But to understand the American media, the first concept to understand is that the central force driving the media in America is the desire to make money: *American media are businesses, vast businesses.* The products of these businesses are information and entertainment." (p. 150—63 words)

_____

_____

_____

_____

Number of words: _____

3. "The media industries, as already discussed, provide information and entertainment. But media can also be used to try to persuade the public, and media can affect the culture. These last two functions of media—*persuasion and transmission of culture*—form the basis of the scholarly studies that address the effects media have on society and the culture in which they operate." (p. 161—61 words)

_____

_____

_____

_____

Number of words: _____

4. "Early media studies analyzed the message in the belief that, once a message was sent, it would be received by everyone the same way. Then studies proved that different people perceived messages differently (described as **selective perception**). This is because everyone brings many variables to each message: family background, interests, and education, for example." (p. 161—54 words)

_____

_____

_____

_____

Number of words: _____

5. "The attempts by scholars to describe media's social and cultural role in society are important because, once identified, the effects can be observed. The questions should be posed so we do not become complacent about

media in our lives, so we do not become immune to the possibility that our culture may be cumulatively affected by the media in ways we cannot yet define." (p. 161—64 words)

_____

_____

_____

_____

Number of words: _____

EXERCISE 4.5

Directions: On a separate sheet of paper, summarize this longer excerpt from the reading. Follow the guidelines on page 88. The original text has 258 words. Try to keep your summary below 90 words, but do not omit any key information. Don't forget to cite your source.

The channels of communication have changed dramatically over the centuries, but the idea that a society will pay to stay informed and entertained is not new. In imperial Rome, people who wanted to know the news paid professional speakers a coin (*gazet*) for the privilege of listening to the speaker announce the day's events. Many early newspapers were called gazettes to reflect this heritage.

The first attempt at written communication began modestly with pictographs. A pictograph is a symbol of an object that is used to convey an idea. If you have ever drawn a heart with an arrow through it, you understand what a pictograph is. The first known pictographs were carved in stone by the Sumerians of Mesopotamia in about 3500 B.C.

The stone in which these pictograph messages were carved served as a medium—a device for transmitting messages. Eventually, messages were imprinted in clay and stored in a primitive version of today's library. These messages weren't very portable, however. Clay tablets didn't slip easily into someone's pockets.

In about 2500 B.C., the Egyptians invented papyrus, a type of paper made from a grasslike plant called sedge. The Greeks perfected parchment, made from goat and sheepskins, in about 200 B.C. By about A.D. 100, before the use of parchment spread throughout Europe, the Chinese had invented paper, but the Europeans didn't start to use paper until more than a thousand years later, about A.D. 1300. The discovery of parchment and then paper meant that storing information became cheaper and easier.

Source: "The Communication Process," from *Media/Impact: An Introduction to Mass Media* (2nd ed.), by Shirley Biagi (p. 21)

EXERCISE 4.6

Directions: Summarize the Soviet Theory, the Authoritarian Theory, the Libertarian Theory, the Social Responsibility Theory, and the Developmental Theory. These are described beginning on page 159 of "The Communication Process." Use these summaries later when you study for the Chapter 4 test.

NOTE: It is generally preferable to use summaries rather than direct quotes in your academic writing (research papers, essay exam answers, etc.). When you summarize, there will be a single writing style; the text will flow better and be easier to read. Use direct quotes when the original wording will have a strong impact.

LEARNING STRATEGY

Managing Your Learning: Summarizing is a good way to check your understanding of a concept.

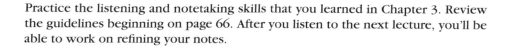

REFINING YOUR LECTURE NOTES

Practice the listening and notetaking skills that you learned in Chapter 3. Review the guidelines beginning on page 66. After you listen to the next lecture, you'll be able to work on refining your notes.

EXERCISE 4.7

Directions: You will hear a lecture entitled "Media Manipulation." Listen and take notes.

EXERCISE 4.8

Directions: Take a minute to try to fill in the gaps in your lecture with the help of your classmates or by asking your instructor specific questions.

LEARNING STRATEGY

Testing Hypotheses: Ask for clarification if information provided in class lectures is confusing.

After you have filled in the gaps in your lecture notes, you can further refine your notes by filling in unknown definitions or information from your textbook in the margin of your notes. You can also add specific information from your reading which seems to relate to points made in the lecture. These relationships could come up in an exam question.

If you have time, summarize each lecture or important parts of the lecture after class. Try to do this while the material is still fresh in your mind. In any case, you should review your notes after class or later in the day before you have a chance to forget the material.

EXERCISE 4.9

Directions: List the points the instructor seemed to stress in the lecture. See if your classmates came to the same conclusions.

1. _____
2. _____
3. _____
4. _____
5. _____

EXERCISE 4.10

Directions: On a separate sheet of paper, summarize the sections of your notes that you listed in Exercise 4.9. You can use these summaries later when you are studying for the Chapter 4 test.

IMPROVING YOUR MEMORY

Reading and notetaking are both active processes. Reviewing and quizzing yourself frequently will help you retain information. These techniques will help to improve your memory. You won't remember much if you just read and reread your textbook and lecture notes. You have to do more than that to commit all the new material to memory. Try the following techniques to help you improve your memory:

1. Make sure you understand the material. Ask for clarification in class, or see your professor during office hours.
2. Review and test yourself frequently on the course material. You know how to form the questions. Practice answering in a variety of ways—out loud, in writing, or with a study partner.
3. Learn your material in meaningful units. Try not to separate related facts. If you understand how the material in your course is related, it will be easier to understand and remember.
4. Organize your material in a meaningful way. Number all lists (reasons, facts, points, etc.) and memorize the number of items to be recalled (e.g., 5 forms of concentration of ownership).
5. Go over your course material from time to time with a study group. You can throw questions back and forth. It's fast and lively.

6. Visualize the new material. Make illustrations, charts, and diagrams. Remember the expression, "A picture is worth a thousand words."

7. Make brief study notes in outline form from your textbook chapters.

8. Paraphrase key points. Your own words are easier to understand and remember.

9. Summarize your lecture notes and readings. You'll be certain that you understand the material, and it's always easier to remember material written in your own words.

10. Short and frequent study sessions are generally more effective than long and infrequent ones.

11. Use *mnemonics.* A mnemonic device is an aid to help you remember something.

  a. An *acronym* is a word formed from the first letters of a compound name or by combining initial letters of parts of words. You can create your own acronyms to help you remember facts. Here are some well-known acronyms.

   WHO = World Health Organization
   radar = radio detecting and ranging

  b. Words taken from sentences can also help you recall information. Underline the most significant words from sentences explaining a concept and learn the list of words. During a test, these words will trigger your memory so that you can recall the whole concept. The following example can help you learn the characteristics of the Authoritarian Theory as described in the chapter by Shirley Biagi.

    First, write brief sentences outlining the information to be learned. Then underline the most significant word in each sentence.
   • License everyone who owned a press.
   • If someone published something that did not favor the government, revoke the license.
   • Review material after it was published.
   • Punish those who published unfavorable material.

    Study the concept and memorize the list of words. When you take the test, the list of words will help you recall the concept.
     —license
     —revoke
     —review
     —punish

    Sometimes you can make an acronym from the first letter(s) of each word to make them even easier to remember.

LEARNING STRATEGY

Remembering New Material: Using mnemonic devices helps you to remember new material.

EXERCISE 4.11

Directions: Form a study group of three or four students. Based on the lecture you just heard, turn the major headings in your notes into questions. Take turns asking those questions of the other members in your group. Ask the same questions more than once. See if one of your classmates answers with additional information or takes a different approach. Be sure to listen for incorrect information and correct or clarify information when necessary.

LEARNING STRATEGY

Remembering New Material: Working in study groups can make practicing new material more enjoyable.

EXERCISE 4.12

Directions: In the box, draw a simple illustration that shows *intrapersonal communication, interpersonal communication,* and *mass communication.* Refer to page 149 in "The Communication Process" and reread the information on these three types of communication before you attempt your illustration. Compare your diagram to those of your classmates to see if you visualized the three types of communication in similar ways.

EXERCISE 4.13

Directions: Practice coming up with memory-enhancing techniques to help you learn the information in this chapter. Refer to "The Communication Process." You can use your answers to help you study for the chapter test.

1. What acronym can help you remember the three elements that are essential to today's concept of mass media: *storability, portability,* and *accessibility*?
2. What does the Libertarian Theory assume? Review page 158. Write brief sentences describing the points of the theory. Then underline the most significant word in each sentence. Make a list of these words.
3. Review the section of the chapter beginning "Who Owns the Media?" on page 151. Define the trend of <u>concentration of ownership</u> and summarize its five forms.
4. Read the section of the chapter beginning "How Does Each Media Industry Work?" on page 153. Make brief study notes in outline form. Show the characteristics of each medium in your notes.

Managing Your Learning: Use a variety of techniques when you review course material to make studying more interesting.

GETTING INVOLVED IN CLASS DISCUSSIONS

In colleges and universities, there are several types of classes. Some classes have a **lecture** format, where the professor does most of the talking. The students in these classes are expected to listen and take notes. They are only occasionally asked to participate. In other classes, the professors will encourage discussion among the students. In a third type, **seminar** classes, the students are expected to do most of the talking. These classes are very small, and all students are expected to participate equally.

EXERCISE 4.14

Directions: Discuss the following questions.

Are students expected to participate actively in classes in your country? Do your professors encourage students to speak out in class? Do you find it difficult to speak in class? Explain your answers.

Speaking in class is difficult at first for many students. The following guidelines may make it a little easier for you to get started:

1. Come to class prepared. Do the reading and assignments in advance. Review your notes from the previous classes. You won't be able to participate, or even ask meaningful questions, if you aren't up to date in your work.
2. If you are unsure about something, you can ask questions during class discussions. Chances are that other students have the same questions in mind. You can also add your own comments at this time.
3. Make sure your comments are clear and short. Never dominate a class discussion.
4. If you are talking to your professor, make eye contact with him or her. If you are talking to the class, move your eyes from student to student. Don't direct your attention to a single student.
5. Try not to deviate from the point or get personal in your comments. Stick to the facts under discussion.
6. Be sure you can back up your comments with facts. Don't get caught in a position where you're unable to prove your point.

7. Don't interrupt when someone else is speaking.
8. Try to take notes during class discussions. A good professor will get the students to produce important information. Information from class discussions could appear on exams.
9. If a professor spends a great deal of discussion time in a certain area or seems especially enthused about something, write in your notes that this is a possible exam question.
10. Concentrate on the discussion and on taking notes. Don't let your mind wander.

EXERCISE 4.15

Directions: Read the following passage carefully. Then answer the questions orally. Some of the answers will not be found in the text. You'll have to think them out. Everyone should try to participate in this discussion. Follow the guidelines above.

> **Who Owns the Media?** To understand the media, it is important to know who owns these important channels of communication. In America, all of the media are privately owned except the Public Broadcasting Service and National Public Radio, which survive on government support and private donations. The annual budget for public broadcasting, however, is less than 3 percent of the amount of money advertisers pay every year to support America's commercial media.
>
> Many family-owned media properties still exist in the United States, but today the trend in the media industries, like other American industries, is for media companies to cluster together in groups. The top ten newspaper chains, for example, own one-fifth of the nation's daily newspapers. This trend is called **concentration of ownership,** and this concentration takes five different forms.
>
> Source: "The Communication Process," from *Media/Impact: An Introduction to Mass Media* (2nd ed.), by Shirley Biagi (p. 9)

1. Who owns the media in the United States? Be specific.
2. How do the Public Broadcasting Service and National Public Radio survive? Are you familiar with PBS and NPR? How does their programming differ from commercial media? If you are not familiar with them, how do you think their programming differs based on their funding sources?
3. What is the trend of concentration of ownership? What are the consequences of this concentration? Who benefits from this type of organization? Who suffers?
4. Which do you think is better, public or private ownership of the media? Why?
5. Who owns the media in your country? Are people in your country generally happy with this ownership? Why or why not?
6. Do you think the quality of the media would be better or worse if its ownership in your country were different? Explain your answer.

Threads

In 1898, Guglielmo Marconi installed the first commercial radio service.

Encyclopedia Americana, 1993

Threads

In 1930, Philo T. Farnsworth developed a new electronic scanning system that made TV pictures suitable for the home.

Encyclopedia Americana, 1993

EXERCISE 4.16

Directions: Based on questions posed by the lecturer and by Shirley Biagi in "The Communication Process," discuss the following issues. Your instructor may ask you to break into small groups for this discussion. Follow the guidelines listed on pages 96–97. Feel free to provide additional information to an answer that one of your classmates has given.

1. Do the owners of the media have too much power in the United States? Explain your answer.
2. Should the government withhold information from the media? Is this ever justified? If the media gets hold of secret government information, are they justified in presenting it to the public? Why or why not?
3. Do the television networks and the film industry have an obligation to provide high-quality entertainment to the public? Explain your answer.
4. Is the public becoming more or less knowledgeable as a result of the trends in mass media? Explain your answer.

LEARNING STRATEGY

Understanding and Using Emotions: Practicing speaking in class makes it easier and less stressful.

SYNTHESIZING COURSE MATERIAL

On page 67, we talked about the importance of learning material in meaningful units and understanding how the material in a course is related. **Synthesizing** is the combining of separate elements to form a coherent whole. Very often, you will have to synthesize course material. For example, you'll have to put material from several sources together to come up with a complete exam answer. Therefore, it is necessary to be aware of the ways in which the information in your course is related.

These relationships are usually obvious in your textbooks. All the material in a chapter is related. The subheadings all give more detailed information about the headings.

EXERCISE 4.17

Directions: Turn to page 150 in "The Communication Process". Complete the outline using the heading and subheadings in the chapter. The topic outline of this chapter makes it easy to see how the sections in the chapter are related.

I. Understanding the Mass Media Industries: Four Key Themes
   A. The Media as Business
      1. _____
      2. _____
      3. _____
   B. _____
      1. _____
   C. _____
      1. _____
      2. _____
      3. _____
      4. _____
      5. _____
   D. _____

EXERCISE 4.18

Directions: Look at the topic outline in Exercise 4.17 and answer the following questions.

1. What are the four key themes discussed in the chapter?
2. How many key issues are discussed in "The Media as Business" section? What are they?
3. How many communication revolutions have there been?
4. How many theories are discussed which show the relationship of the media to government? What are they?

It is also important to see the relationship between the readings and lectures in a course. You have been advised to make notations in your textbook and in your lecture notes when you see a relationship between two ideas or when you see that information which is spoken of briefly in one place is expanded upon in another. Your professor may ask questions on essay exams where you will be expected to **synthesize** information from two or three sources into a single answer on a test.

EXERCISE 4.19

Directions: Look at your lecture notes and "The Communication Process." List topics that are related. Compare your answers with a classmate to see if one of you has come up with a relationship that the other missed.

1. _____
2. _____
3. _____

Preparing for an essay test is different from preparing for an objective test. For objective tests, you have to know many details. However, if you are having trouble recalling the facts, you will see the answer or at least some of the information in the question itself, and that may trigger your memory. If necessary, you can use guessing strategies, which often work.

When studying for essay tests, you have to learn broad concepts, evidence to support these concepts, main ideas, key details, examples, reasons, steps, and so on. You have a blank sheet of paper in front of you. You have to have complete recall of the information. Your essay not only needs to be factually correct but it also has to be clear, well organized, and well written. You will be expected to synthesize information from different sources. You will sometimes be asked to include your opinion, response, or reaction in the answer.

To prepare for *any* test, do the following:

1. Go to class every day, keep up with your reading, and take careful lecture notes.
2. Use the study techniques that you have been practicing. Review your course material frequently throughout the semester.
3. Keep up with new vocabulary.
4. Make note of potential exam questions from your textbook and the lectures.
5. Review the test preparation guidelines on page 78 in Chapter 3.

Reading and Understanding Essay Test Questions

Here is a list of the words most frequently used in the directions of essay tests. Make sure that you understand the directions so that you can write accurate answers.

analyze	examine the individual parts or principles to help understand the whole concept
comment	a statement of fact or opinion
compare	show similarities and/or differences
contrast	show differences
criticize	judge, analyze, and evaluate
critique	a commentary or critical review
define	give the exact meaning
demonstrate	prove by reason or evidence
describe	tell about in detail
determine	explain and come to a conclusion
develop	progress from stage to stage (e.g., earlier to later, simpler to more complex, etc.)
diagram	draw, outline, or explain to show something or clarify a relationship

differentiate	show the differences
discuss	write about something in detail
elaborate	write about something in greater detail; provide further information
enumerate	list; name one by one and describe
evaluate	examine and judge
exemplify	explain and give examples
explain	make a concept clear and comprehensible; offer reasons or a cause
formulate	explain in systematic terms or concepts
illustrate	explain by use of examples, comparisons, etc.
interpret	offer a clear explanation
justify	demonstrate or prove that a concept is just, right, or valid
list	explain item-by-item, sometimes arranged in a particular order; enumerate
outline	describe or summarize
prove	show that something is true or valid by argument or evidence
relate	show a logical or natural association
review	examine again; write a critical report
state	describe; declare
summarize	explain or describe briefly
trace	show the successive stages in development or progress

Essay exam questions often have several parts. Be sure to answer the entire question.

Always follow the directions carefully. Sometimes you will be asked to answer all of the questions. Other times, you will be directed to answer only a portion of them (e.g., "Answer 3 of the 5 questions."). In this case, you will get no extra credit if you answer all the questions, and you will have lost valuable time.

Budgeting Your Time on an Essay Test

You have to budget your time carefully on essay tests. If you run out of time and leave out an entire question, you run the risk of losing 10, 20, or more points. When planning how to budget your time, consider the following:

1. Preview the whole test. Read all the directions carefully before you begin. If you don't understand the directions, ask the professor for clarification.
2. Very often, the professor will give the point value of each question as part of the directions. Spend more time on the questions with higher point values.
3. Some students like to do the easy questions first, some like to do the difficult ones first, and others like to go in order. Do what works best for you.
4. Save time at the end of the test to edit.

EXERCISE 4.20

Directions: Decide how you would budget your time for the following tests. Work with a partner and see if you agree on the best strategy for completing these tests.

Test #1: 50 minutes

Short answer (5 out of 8)	10 points each	50 points
Essay question #1	20 points	20 points
Essay question #2	30 points	30 points
		100 points

How would you budget your time?

_____ minutes to preview the test

_____ minutes to briefly outline your answers

_____ minutes to do short answer questions

　　　　　　　(_____ minutes each)

_____ minutes to do essay question #1

_____ minutes to do essay question #2

_____ minutes to go over your test before handing it in

Total: 50 minutes

In what order would you answer these questions? Why?

Test #2: 90 minutes

5 short answer	3 points each	15 points
Essay question #1	20 points	20 points
Essay question #2	25 points	25 points
Essay question #3	40 points	40 points
		100 points

How would you budget your time?

_____ minutes to preview the test

_____ minutes to briefly outline your answers

_____ minutes to do short answer questions

　　　　　　　(_____ minutes each)

_____ minutes to do essay question #1

_____ minutes to do essay question #2

_____ minutes to do essay question #3

_____ minutes to go over your test before handing it in

Total: 90 minutes

In what order would you answer these questions? Why?

Writing Essay Test Answers

There are a number of techniques that you can use to produce the kind of essay answers that professors look for. Follow these guidelines when you are writing an essay test.

Before you start writing:

1. Come to the exam prepared with pencils, pen, scratch paper, and any other material that your professor has given you permission to use during the test. If you have to write the test on your own paper, use $8\frac{1}{2}$" × 11" paper.
2. Arrive a little early at the test area.
3. Read the entire test and budget your time carefully before you begin to write.
4. If any of your mnemonic devices or illustrations apply to the test questions, write them down quickly on your scratch paper if your professor permits you to do this.
5. Make brief outlines on your scratch paper for each question. (You may decide either to do all your outlines at once or to do one outline and then write the answer.) Your outline will help you organize your answer.

Writing the test:

6. Restate the question in the first sentence of your answer. This will help you to focus on the question. It will also show your professor that you understood the question. There are two ways to restate the question:
   a. Repeat key words from the question in the first sentence of your answer.

      EXAMPLE:

      Question: Compare the Federal Communications Commission (FCC) regulations concerning broadcast ownership now to the pre-1980 regulations.

      First sentence of answer: The Federal Communications Commission regulations concerning broadcast ownership have changed in the following ways since 1980.

   b. Repeat key words from the question and summarize the answer in the first sentence of your answer:

      EXAMPLE:

      Question: Enumerate and discuss the three terms used to describe how people communicate.

      First Sentence of Answer: The three terms used to describe how people communicate are intrapersonal communication, interpersonal communication, and mass communication.

7. Write complete sentences in well-developed paragraphs. Refer to your outline as you write to be sure that your answer is organized and you are not forgetting any important points.

8. Use signal words to organize your answers and to make them clear. (Review pages 57-58)

   EXAMPLE:

   <u>Question</u>: Enumerate and discuss the three terms used to describe how people communicate.

   <u>Answer</u>: The three terms used to describe how people communicate are intrapersonal communication, interpersonal communication, and mass communication. The <u>first</u> term, intrapersonal communication, is the constant communication that we have with ourselves. No other person is involved in this form of communication. <u>For example</u>, the dozens of decisions we make every day usually occur internally. <u>The next type</u> is interpersonal communication—communicating with other people. Any interaction with another person is interpersonal. The <u>third</u> type of communication is mass communication—communication by one person to a large number of people. Mass communication occurs through the use of print (newspaper, books, and magazines) and electronics (television, radio, and computers).

9. Support the points you make in your essay with specific examples, proof, or citations.

10. Don't pad your answer. Stick to the point. Your professor will not be impressed if you write several paragraphs (or several pages) that may be factually correct but do not address the question.

11. If you have written a long essay, conclude your answer with a brief summary of the facts. A formal conclusion is not necessary for a short essay.

12. Pay attention to your time limit.

13. If you don't know the answer, don't leave a blank. Try to get something on your paper. You may get a few points.

14. If you run out of time, quickly copy the remainder of your outline on to your test paper to show your professor the direction your answer would have taken had you had time to finish. You might get some points for this.

After you finish writing:

15. Save time at the end to edit your test. Check it over to make sure that it is factually correct and that you haven't left out any important information. Also, check it for clarity, organization, grammar, and spelling.

16. Make sure each question is clearly numbered.

17. Put your name on each sheet of paper.

18. Number each page.

It is essential that your essays be well organized, concise, to the point, and legible. Your professor has a lot of exams to read. Be considerate of that fact when you are writing.

LEARNING STRATEGY

Managing Your Learning: Knowing what to expect on a test helps you to get a good grade.

EXERCISE 4.21

Directions: Review the exam questions written below. Then complete all four parts of the instructions: (1) Circle the direction words, (2) write the first sentence of the answer, remembering to restate the question (and perhaps summarizing the whole answer in your first sentence), (3) tell how you would organize the answer, and (4) indicate possible signal words you would use throughout your answer. (Refer to pages 57–58 for information on organization and signal words.) The page numbers from the chapter are given to help you complete the first sentence. **(You do not have to write complete answers to these questions.)**

1. Enumerate and describe the political organization of media systems as described by Fred S. Siebert in his book *Four Theories of the Press.* (p. 159)

   First sentence of answer: _____

   _____

   Organization: _____

   Signal Words: _____

2. In 1980 the FCC under the Reagan administration deregulated the broadcast media. Prove that this deregulation contributed to the unprecedented buying and selling of television networks and radio stations in the 1980s. (p. 152)

   First sentence of answer: _____

   _____

   Organization: _____

   Signal Words: _____

3. Fewer and fewer media properties are owned by individuals. More often they are owned by groups. Summarize the five different forms of concentration of ownership. (p. 151)

   First sentence of answer: _____

   _____

   Organization: _____

   Signal Words: _____

4. Although the movie industry is still bringing in huge profits, it is currently undergoing major changes. Contrast the industry today to a decade ago. (pp. 154–155)

   First sentence of answer: _____

   _____

   Organization: _____

   Signal Words: _____

5. People have always wanted to stay informed; however, the means of providing information to the people have changed dramatically over time. Trace the channels of communication from the use of pictographs through the use of computers. Give specific examples. (p. 156)

First sentence of answer: _____

_____

Organization: _____

Signal Words: _____

Editing Essay Test Answers

Give yourself enough time to proofread your answers before you hand in your test. If you find that you need to add a word or two, you can use a caret (∧). If you have to add a sentence or two, put an asterisk (✳) at the appropriate spot, put another asterisk at the bottom of the page, and write the additional information. If you have to cross anything out, do it neatly.

> 1. The three terms used to describe how people communicate are intrapersonal communication, interpersonal communication, and mass communication. The first term, intrapersonal communication, is the constant communication which we have within ourselves.✳ For example, the dozens of ∧decisions made everyday usually occur internally.
>
> ✳ No other person is involved in this form of communication.

Guessing Test Questions in Advance

You have already practiced guessing test questions in advance. To review, ask yourself:

1. What has been emphasized in the course?
2. What has been spoken about in the greatest detail?

3. What did the professor spend the most time on?
4. What did the professor seem to be most enthused about?
5. What important relationships are there between your textbook and your lecture notes?
6. What are the key points in your textbook? (If your textbook has study questions, consider them carefully.)
7. What information was covered in review sessions?

LEARNING STRATEGY

Managing Your Learning: Use clues given throughout the semester to try to guess test questions in advance.

EXERCISE 4.22

Directions: In Exercise 4.9 on page 93, you listed five areas the instructor seemed to stress in the lecture. Now predict six possible exam questions based on the lecture, the reading, and any relationships that you see between them. Compare your questions with your classmates to see if you come up with similar questions.

1. _____
2. _____
3. _____
4. _____
5. _____
6. _____

Preparing Practice Answers

EXERCISE 4.23

Directions: Make an outline for each of the questions you came up with in Exercise 4.22. Then write practice answers for these questions. Be sure to follow the guidelines in this chapter. You can use these answers to help you study for the upcoming essay test.

 **TAKING AN ESSAY TEST**

EXERCISE 4.24

Directions: Review "The Communication Process" and the lecture. You will have an essay test on this material.

EXERCISE 4.25

Directions: Discuss the following questions.

Were you able to complete all of the work presented in this chapter? Do you feel that you were adequately prepared for the test? Of the material presented in this chapter, what do you still find difficult? Are you satisfied with the grade you received on the test? How could you improve your performance the next time?

SUMMARY

In Chapter 4, you had the opportunity to practice some more advanced academic skills. A great amount of preparation is required for all university classes.

ON YOUR OWN	IN CLASS
Keeping Up with Your Work	
Reading and Preparing Study Notes	
Summarizing	
Refining Your Notes	
Improving Your Memory	
	Getting Involved in Class Discussions
Synthesizing Course Material	
Preparing for an Essay Test	
	Reading and Understanding Essay Test Questions
	Budgeting Your Time on an Essay Test
	Writing Essay Test Answers
	Editing Essay Test Answers
Guessing Test Questions in Advance	
Preparing Practice Answers	
	Taking an Essay Test

Working on a Group Project

In this chapter you will:

- work on a group project.
- give an oral presentation.
- think about prioritizing your class work.
- examine your academic strengths and weaknesses.

You are going to begin to work on a group project that will require doing research in the library and working cooperatively with your partners. You can practice many of the skills that you learned in this course while you are completing your project. In addition, each group will give an oral presentation to the class.

Discuss the following questions with your classmates.

1. Students generally do their schoolwork independently, whereas people in the workplace frequently work cooperatively with a group. Do you prefer to work individually or in a group? Explain your answer.
2. Have you ever done a group project in school? If you answered yes, describe your project to the class.
3. Have you ever given an oral presentation in English to a group? If you answered yes, describe your presentation.
4. Do you feel that you are good at convincing others of your point of view? What skills are necessary to argue persuasively?
5. At the end of the semester when you are very busy, how do you prioritize your work?

NOTE: All excerpts in this chapter have been taken from "Comparison of Personality and Social Behavior" in *Gender: Stereotypes and Roles,* (3rd ed.) by Susan A. Basow. (Copyright © 1992 by Brooks/Cole Publishing Co. Reprinted by permission.) This reading selection can be found on page 163. Before starting to work with this material, consider the following questions.

EXERCISE 5.1

Directions: Write about or discuss the following questions.

Do you think that males and females communicate differently? How does verbal communication differ between genders? How does nonverbal communication differ? Why do you think these differences occur?

WORKING WITH A GROUP

Your instructor is going to assign a group project to the class. General instructions will be given now, and more detailed instructions will be given as the project progresses. This project is a multistep process. You have to complete each step in order to receive credit. Pay attention to the details of the instructions and to the due dates. Remember that the other members in your group are depending on you to do your part.

Understanding the Assignment

Academic speaking and writing assignments fall into two categories: **expository** and **persuasive.** Expository speeches and papers inform, instruct, or describe. Persuasive speeches and papers argue a point or try to change the point of view of the listeners or readers. Make sure you know what approach you are expected to take when you are given an assignment.

When professors assign research papers and other projects, they usually give very detailed instructions on how to complete the task. Be sure you understand the instructions because these assignments will usually account for a large percentage of your grade.

You are going to begin working on a group project. Follow your instructor's directions for every step of the assignment. If you don't understand any portion of the instructions, be sure to ask for clarification.

The following is an overview of the entire project. Your instructor will either collect papers or have conferences with the groups on the due dates. All parts of the project will be evaluated and graded. More detailed instructions will be given as the project progresses. The project will be divided into five parts.

1. **Topic proposal:** Each group will choose a general topic and then generate ideas, by brainstorming, about ways to narrow the topic. You will give a topic proposal to your instructor. You will refine this proposal further as you learn more about your topic and develop new insights.

2. **Preliminary research:** After you have narrowed your topic, group members will go to the library to do preliminary research. You can go individually and have each group member look at the whole topic; or you can divide the research among the group members and have each one look at some aspect of the topic. Write down your sources and take notes on 3" × 5" cards as you do your research. As you learn more about your topic, think about what you want to describe or prove about it. Share your information with the group.

3. **Thesis statement and brief outline:** After you have done preliminary research, you'll be able to revise the topic that you presented in your proposal. Make sure your topic is not too general. The group will write out the revised topic and tell what they want to describe or prove about this topic. This is the **thesis statement.** In addition, write a brief outline indicating how your topic will be presented. At this time, you will divide the task and determine what part of the speech each member will present to the class.

4. **Revised thesis statement and detailed outline:** The groups will revise their thesis statements, and each member will outline his or her part of the speech. Then each group will get together and review all sections for clarity, coherence, and completeness. Each member will practice giving his or her part of the speech to the other members in the group.

5. **Oral presentation:** Each group will give an oral presentation to the class. The instructor will tell you how long each group will have to speak. A brief question-and-answer session will follow each presentation.

EXERCISE 5.2

Directions: Think about the information on the group project that your instructor has given you so far, and write down any questions that come to mind. Compare your questions with those of your classmates and see if you have similar concerns. Then ask your instructor the questions. Make sure you get the information you need. Ask questions as they arise throughout the project.

1. _____

2. _____

3. _____

4. _____

LEARNING STRATEGY

Testing Hypotheses: Ask for clarification if instructions are unclear.

Meeting Deadlines

When a **deadline** or **due date** is given for any assignment, you are expected to complete your work by that time. You will usually receive a lower grade if your work is handed in late. Here is the schedule for your group project. Your instructor will give you the due dates. Be sure to fill them in accurately and refer to these dates regularly while you're working on the project.

Step	Due Date	Point Value
1. Topic proposal	_____	20 points
2. Preliminary research (notes and sources)	_____	20 points
3. Thesis statement and brief outline	_____	20 points
4. Revised thesis statement and detailed outline	_____	20 points
5. Oral presentation	_____	20 points
	Total	100 points

Two grades will be given upon completion of the project. Each group will be graded according to the accumulated points in the five steps of the project. Individual group members will be graded on their portion of the oral presentation. The criteria for evaluation will be discussed in detail later.

In Chapter 2, it was mentioned that you should have a good reason for choosing a research topic. You should have some prior knowledge about it or a special interest in it. Research projects generally take a long time to complete. Try to find a topic that will hold your interest.

EXERCISE 5.3

Directions: If your instructor allows you to choose your own topic, complete the following questionnaire to help you determine your areas of interest.

I. What do you plan to major in in college? (List several disciplines that interest you if you are still undecided.)

    A. _____

    B. _____

    C. _____

II. What world events (past or present) interest you?

    A. _____

    B. _____

    C. _____

III. List people (past or present) or groups of people (indigenous, ethnic, political, counter-culture, etc.; past or present) who interest you.

    A. _____

    B. _____

    C. _____

IV. List any other topics (past, present, or future) that interest you.

    A. _____

    B. _____

    C. _____

    D. _____

    E. _____

IT WORKS!
Learning Strategy:
Having Prior
Knowledge of Your
Research Topic

The topics you have listed above are probably very general. Although you are in the very early stages of your research, it's not too soon to think about how you can go about narrowing these topics.

EXERCISE 5.4

Directions: Form groups of two or three students. You may want to work with specific classmates because you share common interests (e.g., you are planning to pursue the same major in college), you have similar backgrounds (e.g., you come from the same country), you share common interests outside of school (e.g., films, music, art, etc.), or you simply enjoy working together. Compare your questionnaires with others in your class to help you choose your partner(s). Your instructor may want to assist you in assigning groups.

Each group will complete a research project. The project will be broken down into five parts. You have already recorded the due dates. You will receive credit for each part. Each individual stage of the process will be discussed in detail in class. If you skip a step in the process, your group will lose 20 points.

EXERCISE 5.5

Directions: Get together with your group and decide what general topic you would like to work on. Begin preliminary discussions on your topic. At this early stage, your topic will be very general.

NOTE: Avoid topics that are too current. You may not be able to find adequate material in the library or in the news, and current events can change dramatically overnight. Also, choose topics for which there will be adequate resources in the library. If you choose a topic concerning an event or situation in your own country, consider that the library may have very little information on the subject. Your instructor can advise you in these areas.

Brainstorming

Brainstorming is a way to generate ideas. Write down your general topic and then write down all the related subtopics that you can think of. The purpose of brainstorming is to get a variety of ideas down on paper. Don't judge the feasibility of your ideas at this time.

There are two ways to brainstorm. You can either **list** your ideas or you can **map** them. Here are examples of these two techniques using the general topic, "Verbal Communication," discussed in the chapter by Susan A. Basow on page 163.

Listing:

Verbal Communication

Females
better listeners
interrupted more
more personal
polite
ask questions
use qualifiers

Males
dominate conversations
talk more
joke
slang
more familiar
use first names

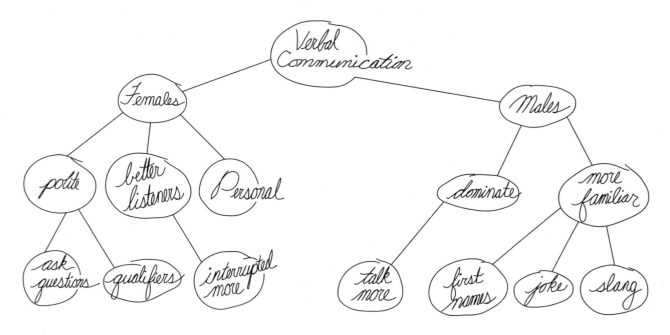

LEARNING STRATEGY

Personalizing: Use your personal experience and prior knowledge to help generate new ideas.

EXERCISE 5.6

Directions: On a separate sheet of paper, brainstorm the following general topics. Use listing for one and mapping for the other. Work with your group. When you finish, your instructor may ask you to share your ideas with the class.

Topic #1: American Culture
Topic #2: Mass Media

EXERCISE 5.7

Directions: Brainstorm with your group to generate ideas on the topic you chose in Exercise 5.5 for your oral presentation. It's important that each member of the group participate in this activity.

EXERCISE 5.8

Directions: Look at the various ideas that your group generated during the brainstorming activity in Exercise 5.7. Come to a consensus within your group as to which area of your general topic you would like to pursue.

EXERCISE 5.9

Directions: Each group will write a brief proposal on the topic it chose in Exercise 5.8. Tell why this topic interests you and how you intend to approach it. The proposal should be only two or three sentences long. Be sure that all group members' names are on the proposal before it's turned in. Your instructor will look at the proposals and either offer suggestions or tell the group to go ahead with the project. Turn in your proposals by the due date.

EXERCISE 5.10

Directions: While the groups are brainstorming and working on their proposals, each group will meet individually with the instructor to present the topic and to get advice and feedback. This is a good opportunity to ask questions.

EXERCISE 5.11

Directions: Go to the library and do some preliminary reading on your topic. Look at at least four sources. Use books, newspapers, or journals. Take notes on 3" × 5" cards. Use a new card for each book or article. On one side of the card, take brief notes as you do your research; on the other side, give the following bibliographic information:

For books:
1. Author
2. Title
3. Year of Publication
4. Page numbers of useful information
5. Call number

For periodicals:
1. Author
2. Title of article
3. Title of publication
4. Date of publication
5. Page numbers of article
6. Form
7. Call number

As you find material on your topic, read and take notes. This is your opportunity to learn about your topic and to decide how you want to present it. As you do your preliminary research, share your information with your group. Continue to read and learn more about your topic. Meet frequently with your group to discuss ideas.

Your instructor may not check back with you until the next due date. If you have any questions in the meantime, you can see your instructor during class time or office hours. Your instructor will have a conference with your group to go over your notes on the due date.

IT WORKS!
Learning Strategy:
Taking
Careful Notes

NOTE: If you are unable to find adequate material at this early stage of your research, you'll have to reconsider your topic. You may either want to take a different approach to the same topic or change your topic. Try not to change your topic completely because all of your work will have been wasted. If you are having trouble at this stage, your instructor can probably advise you. Don't hesitate to ask for help.

Writing a Thesis Statement

The next step in the assignment is to come up with a **thesis statement** and a brief outline. Now that your group has chosen a topic and narrowed it, it is time to decide what you want to describe or prove about your topic. Your topic plus a statement telling what you want to describe, prove, argue, or evaluate is the thesis statement. Look at the following example.

General topic:
Verbal Communication

Narrower topic:
Verbal Communication Between Males and Females

Thesis statement:
That males are more dominant and direct in their verbal communication is a reflection of how they perceive themselves in society.

EXERCISE 5.12

Directions: Look again at the brainstorming activity in Exercise 5.6. Work with your group to write a narrower topic and a thesis statement for both of the general topics.

General topic #1:
American Culture

Narrower topic:

_____

Thesis statement:

_____

_____

_____

General topic #2:
Mass Media

Narrower topic:

_____

Thesis statement:

_____

_____

_____

EXERCISE 5.13

Directions: Work with your group. On a separate sheet of paper, come up with a narrower topic and a thesis statement for your topic. Then write a brief outline indicating the areas you want to cover in your presentation. Use your research notes to help you complete your outline. Be sure this exercise is completed by the due date.

EXERCISE 5.14

IT WORKS!
Learning Strategy:
Having Prior
Knowledge of Your
Research Topic

Directions: After your instructor has approved your thesis statement and outline, assign sections of the outline to each member of the group. Each group member will be responsible for doing the final research in his or her area and then for presenting this portion of the material to the class orally. If you have material that another group member could use, be sure to share it.

USING BOOKS AS REFERENCES

Whenever you purchase a textbook or use a book or article for research, examine it from beginning to end before you begin to use it. It may contain valuable information that you did not expect to find. You are already familiar with this textbook because you have been using the glossary and the appendices. You should survey all your textbooks to see if they can be used as reference sources.

When you use books and articles for research, always check the publication date. Avoid using out-of-date publications. When you use books, check the table of contents to get an overview of the information found in the book. Use the index to help you find information in the book quickly. Check books and articles for **bibliographies.** They will help you to find more information on the same topic.

EXERCISE 5.15

Directions: Choose a book that you are using in one of your other courses and answer the following questions.

1. Title: _____

2. Author: _____

3. Turn to the title page. Is the author affiliated with a college or university? (Look below the author's name.)

4. Look at the back of the title page. What is the publication date? (Get into the habit of looking at the publication date on all books and articles so that you can be sure that you are using up-to-date material. This is especially important when you are doing academic research.)

5. Look at the table of contents. How is the book organized?

6. Look at the first chapter.

   a. How are the chapters divided?

   b. What type of illustrations are there?

   c. Is there a summary at the beginning or end of the chapter?

   d. Is there a bibliography at the end of the chapter?

   e. Are there study questions at the beginning or end of the chapter?

   f. Does the author use boldface print or italics to make important vocabulary or concepts stand out?

7. Look at the end of the book. If there are appendices, what information do they include? Is there a glossary? How is the index organized?

IT WORKS!
Learning Strategy:
Looking for
Answers in
References

WRITING ONE-SENTENCE SUMMARIES

There will be times when you will want to reduce a longer text to a single sentence—a one-sentence summary. To do this, follow the summarizing guidelines on page 88. In a one-sentence summary, however, you will give little more than the author, the source, and the main idea or thesis statement. Sometimes you can show the organization of the original text (comparison/contrast, cause/effect, etc.) by using signal words and the author's tone or attitude by your choice of introductory verbs ("The author *suggests,*" "The author *insists,*" "The author *argues,*" etc.).

Look at the following paragraph and one-sentence summary.

The term *personality* refers to the distinctive character of an individual, which includes traits, behaviors, emotions and thoughts, whereas *temperament* refers to emotional mood or disposition only. Both areas have been assumed to show gender differences. Most personality theorists, however, emphasize individual, rather than sex-specific differences. Psychodynamic theorists, starting with Freud, are exceptions.

Source: "Comparisons of Personality and Social Behavior" from *Gender: Stereotypes and Roles* (3rd ed.), by Susan A. Basow (p. 54)

Susan A. Basow in her book, *Gender: Stereotypes and Roles*, states that differences among individuals and, to a lesser extent, between genders appear in both *personality* and *temperament.*

EXERCISE 5.16

Directions: Write one-sentence summaries for the following passages. Include the author (Susan A. Basow) and the source (*Gender: Stereotypes and Roles,* 3rd ed.) for the first one. The others will be the same, so it is not necessary to cite the source each time.

1. "Many social behaviors and the way they are measured change as a function of age. Thus, it is important to take the age of the participants into account in comparing studies and in drawing conclusions. For example, research done with college students, generally aged 18 to 22, may not accurately generalize to all adults. Similarly, findings from research based on male participants may not accurately be generalized to females, as many researchers have done." (p. 164)

_____

_____

_____

2. "It is important to recognize the tremendous range of individual differences in the area of personality and social behavior. Such differences overshadow any gender-based ones. Thus, clear-cut differences between males and females are difficult to find and of little use in predicting an individual's performance." (p. 164)

_____

_____

_____

3. "With gender stereotypes being as pervasive as they are, it is not surprising that most people see themselves as behaving in gender-appropriate ways. Whether or not they actually behave this way is a different matter. This question will be the focus of the rest of the chapter. Even when behavioral differences are found, they are as or more likely to be due to situational factors, differential learning opportunities, or societal rewards as to differences in personality." (p. 165)

_____

_____

_____

4. "Overall, the type of verbal communication typical of men (verbal dominance, direct statements, limited intimate self-disclosure) reflects men's greater societal dominance and their concerns with power and competition. Men use talk to negotiate and maintain their higher status. Reciprocally, the type of verbal communication typical of women (listening, qualifying, politeness, personal self-disclosure) reflects women's relative subordination and greater interpersonal involvement. Women use talk to signal support and to maintain relationships." (p. 171)

_____

_____

_____

5. "In sum, females communicate feelings verbally and nonverbally more than males. In contrast, males communicate dominance and power more than females. These communication patterns seem to serve the different roles assigned men and women—interpersonal and agentic, respectively. Communication styles appear to be learned and are related to both sex-typed characteristics and social status." (p. 174)

_____

_____

_____

_____

IT WORKS!
Learning Strategy:
Rephrasing
New Material

KNOWING YOUR AUDIENCE

Whenever you give a speech or write a paper, you have to consider your audience or your readers. This will help you to determine the type of material you will present and the manner in which you will present it. Ask yourself the following questions about the people who will be receiving the information:

1. Will the listeners or readers be interested in the topic?
2. Are they knowledgeable about the subject matter?
3. What countries or cultures are represented in the audience?
4. What is the percentage of males and females?
5. What is their age range?

EXERCISE 5.17

Directions: Discuss the following questions.

Why is it important to consider the points listed above before you give your speech? If you were giving a speech on "Verbal Communication Between Females and Males" for the two audiences shown on the chart below, how would you modify the material so that it would be appropriate and interesting for each group?

Topic: Verbal Communication Between Females and Males	
Characteristics of Group #1	**Characteristics of Group #2**
A university-level linguistics class	A class of high school students
All of the students are native speakers of English	Many international students are in the group
The audience is about 85% female	The audience is about 50% male and 50% female

EXERCISE 5.18

Directions: Your group has chosen a thesis statement, divided the task, and completed the necessary research. Now you have to come up with a final thesis statement. This statement may not change from your earlier one, or you may want to refine it somewhat. After you have settled on your final thesis statement, write a detailed outline of the points to be covered in your oral presentation. Keep your time limit in mind when outlining your speech. After each group member finishes his or her section, put the entire outline together to make sure that the sections flow properly. Work on this outline until you are satisfied with it. Hand your revised thesis statement and detailed outline in to your instructor by the due date.

EXERCISE 5.19

Directions: Your instructor may want to have a conference with each group while you are working on your outlines. Use this opportunity to ask further questions and to get advice.

THINKING CRITICALLY

Critical thinking is the ability to analyze information effectively from one or more perspectives. It is the ability to evaluate and judge the validity, correctness, value, and effectiveness of a concept. Critical thinking enables you to understand material and to present your own ideas effectively. You have been practicing your critical thinking skills throughout this course. For example, you have:

1. asked questions to ensure your understanding of instructions or concepts;
2. distinguished the main idea, the key details, and the less important details in your reading and lectures;
3. analyzed a text in order to write an accurate summary or paraphrase;
4. gone beyond the issues stated in your reading and lectures in order to get involved in class discussions;
5. looked at the relationships between material in your texts and lectures and synthesized this material on tests and in class discussions;
6. analyzed objective test questions to eliminate wrong answers;
7. predicted essay exam questions.

Another important critical thinking skill is the ability to make **inferences.** Making an inference is sometimes called "reading between the lines." The listener or the reader has to interpret information that is not directly stated by the speaker or the author. The listener or reader comes to certain conclusions based on the given information.

EXERCISE 5.20

Directions: Read the following excerpt from *Gender: Stereotypes and Roles,* by Susan A. Basow, and then answer the questions. Your instructor may ask you to work with a partner.

Verbal Communication

Overall, males tend to dominate verbally and females tend to listen. Contradicting the "talkative female" stereotype, Henley and others (for example, Aries, 1987; Lakoff, 1975) have found that males talk more and for longer periods of time than females. Males interrupt other speakers more, control the topic of conversation more, make more jokes, speak less in standard English (that is, they use slang more), and more often use a familiar form of address (first name, "honey") when talking to a female than would a female talking to a male. Females talk at a higher pitch, allow themselves to be interrupted more, listen more, and disclose more personal information to others. Women more than men use tag questions ("It's hot, isn't it?"), qualifiers ("maybe," "I guess"), and compound requests ("Won't you close the window?" rather than "Close the window").

Source: "Comparisons of Personality and Social Behavior" from *Gender: Stereotypes and Roles* (3rd ed.), by Susan A. Basow (p. 58)

Threads

Mouth, n. In man, the gateway to the soul; in woman, the outlet of the heart.

Ambrose Bierce,
The Devil's Dictionary

First, list the verbal communication styles stated in the text.

Females	Males

Then analyze the paragraph and consider what these speech styles seem to indicate about males and females in this culture. Use your critical thinking skills. This information is not given in the text. You have to figure it out based on the information that is given.

Females are:	Males are:

Forming Concepts: Making inferences can help you to figure out the full meaning of a new concept.

ARGUING PERSUASIVELY

In order to argue your point persuasively, you have to be able to support your point of view. Be sure you can back up what you are trying to prove with specific citations, examples, statistics, or studies. Use signal words to argue your point clearly.

EXERCISE 5.21

Directions: Continue reading the passage on "Verbal Communication" from *Gender: Stereotypes and Roles,* by Susan A. Basow.

VERBAL COMMUNICATION

Overall, males tend to dominate verbally and females tend to listen. Contradicting the "talkative female" stereotype, Henley and others (for example, Aries, 1987; Lakoff, 1975) have found that males talk more and for longer periods of time than females. Males interrupt other speakers more, control the topic of conversation more, make more jokes, speak less in standard English (that is, they use slang more), and more often use a familiar form of address (first name, "honey") when talking to a female than would a female talking to a male. Females talk at a higher pitch, allow themselves to be interrupted more, listen more, and disclose more personal information to others. Women more than men use tag questions ("It's hot, isn't it?"), qualifiers ("maybe," "I guess"), and compound requests ("Won't you close the window?" rather than "Close the window"). These three speech style differences are assumed to indicate a lack of assertiveness and more politeness on the part of females. Indeed, women are expected to be polite in their speech, regardless of the gender of the person addressed or the content of the speech (Kemper, 1984). In contrast, males are expected to modify their speech as a function of the gender-appropriateness of the content and the gender of the addressee. For example, it is rarely all right for women to use profanity, but men can use it as long as they don't use it with women. The use of profanity by males appears to demonstrate a degree of social power that women do not have (Selnow, 1985).

These gendered linguistic patterns appear early in life and increase in frequency with age. Even among preschoolers, males tend to talk more, initiate more topics, and use more attention-getting speech devices than their female peers (Austin, Selehi, & Leffler, 1987; Cook, Fritz, McCornack, & Visperas, 1985). In contrast, young girls' speech uses more conversation facilitators and reinforcers than boys' speech. Research on parental directives to young children suggests that children learn these different linguistic styles from their parents (Bellinger & Gleason, 1982). For example, fathers appear to issue more direct commands than mothers ("Put the screw in"), and mothers appear to issue more indirect requests than fathers ("Can you put the screw in?"). Cross-cultural research confirms that gender differences in language use, although fairly universal, are socially constructed (Philips, Steele, & Tanz, 1987).

Differences in content of conversation are not clear because males and females often engage in different activities and occupations. Content differences are also unclear because content of conversation appears to depend not only on the gender of the speaker but also on the gender of the listener (Haas, 1981; J.A. Hall & Braunwald, 1981). Among White middle-class children, boys talk more about sports to both boys and girls, and girls talk to girls more about school, identity, and wishing and needing. When girls talk to boys, they are more verbally compliant and they laugh more. When boys talk to girls, they use more direct requests. College women talk more frequently about a third person than do college men, but there is no gender difference in the frequency of derogatory remarks about that person (Levin & Arluke, 1985). In general, males more often are talked about by both sexes, perhaps a reflection of their greater importance or interest.

With respect to self-disclosure of intimate information, such as personality and bodily matters, women are more self-disclosing than men (Balswick, 1988; Derlega, Durham, Gockel, & Sholis, 1981; C.T. Hill & Stull, 1987). However, when personal topics are considered neutral, such as tactfulness, or masculine, such as aggressiveness, no gender difference regularly appears. With respect to feelings, men are less expressive of positive emotions than negative ones (Saurer & Eisler, 1990).

Source: "Comparisons of Personality and Social Behavior" from
Gender: Stereotypes and Roles (3rd ed.), by Susan A. Basow (p. 58)

You are going to conduct a debate based on the information in the reading you have just completed. Use your critical thinking skills to prepare for the debate. The debate teams will argue the question: Who communicates more effectively: males or females?

Debate rules:

1. Divide the class into two groups. Each team will present an opposing point of view.

Team #1's argument:
Females communicate more effectively than males.

Team #2's argument:
Males communicate more effectively than females.

2. With your group, list all the reasons you can find to support your position. Use the text and your critical thinking skills to help support your argument.
3. Assign each member of the team one or two of the reasons determined in #2. The team members will argue these points.
4. When both teams are prepared, place your chairs in two rows so that the teams are lined up and facing each other.
5. The debate will proceed according to the following rules. Your instructor will determine the time limit that each speaker will have.
   a. A member of Team #1 will present his or her argument.
   b. Any member of Team #2 can dispute this argument.
   c. Any member from Team #1 can defend Team #1's position.
   d. The cycle begins again with Team #2 presenting its first argument, and so on.

NOTE: You do not necessarily have to believe in the point of view that your team is presenting in order to argue persuasively.

To conclude this exercise, the whole class should take a few minutes to discuss the debate and to comment on which points were argued the most persuasively and why they were persuasive.

EXERCISE 5.22

Directions: Watch a news, interview, or information show on TV or listen to one on the radio. Note the name of the program, the name of the speaker or speakers, and the topic under discussion. Take brief notes as you listen. After you finish listening, summarize your notes. Then write a brief paragraph answering the following questions:

1. Was the speaker using expository or persuasive speech?
2. What techniques did the speaker use to convey his or her information clearly?
3. Was this person an effective speaker? Why or why not?

Your instructor may ask you to report this information to the class.

COMPLETING THE PROJECT

While preparing your speech, follow these guidelines:

1. Use your own words as much as possible in your oral presentation. Summarize and paraphrase as necessary. (Cite your sources.)
2. Use signal words so that your ideas are well organized, clear, and easy to follow. (Review pp. 57-58.)
3. Pay attention to your time limit. You may have to take out information if your speech is too long.
4. Support your points with specific examples, statistics, studies, and so on. (Cite your sources.)
5. Do not memorize your speech. Make a brief outline on 3" × 5" cards. Refer to these notes from time to time while you are speaking. Do not read your notes. (You should be well enough prepared for your speech so that you don't have to read your notes.)
6. Pay attention to your grammar, vocabulary, and pronunciation. If you have any language-related questions, ask your instructor before you give your presentation.
7. Make eye contact with your audience. Move your eyes from person to person during your speech.

EXERCISE 5.23

Directions: After your revised thesis statement and detailed outline have been approved by your instructor, the group members will put the sections of their presentation together so that the material flows smoothly. Add transitions and signal words where necessary. Work on this until you are satisfied with the results.

EXERCISE 5.24

Directions: Practice giving your speeches with your group. Time your speeches and make sure you don't go over the time limit. Try to anticipate the kinds of questions your classmates will ask during the question-and-answer session so that you'll be prepared. Ask these questions to the other members of the group to practice.

When you are rehearsing your speeches, consider the following questions to help you to evaluate each other. This will help you to fine-tune your speeches.

The group:

1. Is the group well prepared?
2. Is there an introduction?
3. Is the thesis statement clearly stated at the beginning of the presentation?
4. Is the speech well organized and coherent?
5. Are the ideas presented clearly?
6. Do the speakers use appropriate signal words?
7. Does the topic flow smoothly from speaker to speaker?
8. Is there a conclusion?
9. Does the group stay within the time limit?
10. Are the members of the group well prepared for the question-and-answer session?

The individual group members:

1. Is the group member well prepared?
2. Is the speaker making adequate eye contact with the audience?
3. Is the audience able to hear the speaker?
4. Is the speaker's style relaxed and natural?
5. Is the speaker able to give the presentation without reading his or her notes?
6. Is the speaker's use of language correct (vocabulary, grammar, and pronunciation)?
7. Are the ideas presented clearly?

LEARNING STRATEGY

Managing Your Learning: Look for opportunities to practice with partners.

EXERCISE 5.25

Directions: While students are practicing their presentations, each group will have the last conference with the instructor. You can ask any final questions at this time.

Presenting Your Project to the Class

Your group should be prepared for its oral presentation by the date on your schedule. The audience will take notes while you speak. There will be a short question-and-answer session after you finish.

EXERCISE 5.26

Directions: Students should take notes while other groups are giving their presentations. This will give you a chance to practice notetaking and will also help you to remember key points other groups made in their presentations. Your notes will help to remind you which questions to ask during the question-and-answer session. After all groups have completed their presentations, write a brief summary of each speech from the information in your notes.

EXERCISE 5.27

Directions: Discuss the following questions.

After the presentations are completed, each group should take a few minutes so that the members can evaluate their own work. What was good about your group's presentation? What do you think were its weak areas?

SETTING PRIORITIES

The end of the semester can be traumatic even for the most conscientious students. Everything happens at once: research papers are due, final projects are due, and final exams are scheduled for almost all of your classes. In addition, you often have to begin preparing for the next semester: decide on courses, make living arrangements, and so on. How do you prioritize? Sometimes there is no real answer to this question, and often students look back after the semester ends and wonder how they got through it. The only valid advice is to repeat what has been said throughout this course:

- Keep up with your work.
- Review all your course material frequently throughout the semester.
- Start to prepare for tests and projects early.

EXERCISE 5.28

Directions: List all your end-of-semester projects and exams and their corresponding dates. When did you start to prepare for these exams and projects? Have you run into any problems getting all of your work done? How could you have avoided these pitfalls?

Project or exam	Due date or date of exam	Date you started to prepare

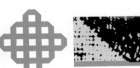

ANALYZING YOUR ACADEMIC STRENGTHS AND WEAKNESSES

The next time you attempt the study skills you learned in this course, you will probably be doing them in a university course for academic credit toward your degree. It's time to think about your academic strengths and weaknesses and to work toward improving your weak areas while taking full advantage of your strong areas.

EXERCISE 5.29

Directions: Discuss the following questions.

Were you able to complete all of the work presented in this chapter? Do you feel that you were adequately prepared for your oral presentation? Of the material presented in this chapter, what do you still find difficult? Are you satisfied with the grade you received on your group project? How could you have improved your performance?

EXERCISE 5.30

Directions: Discuss the following topics.

Look over the skills that you have had the chance to practice in this course. Think about your future as a student in an American college or university.

I. List the areas in which you feel confident.

    A. _____

    B. _____

    C. _____

II. List areas that are still difficult for you and write possible ways to improve these areas.

    A. Problem: _____

        1. Solution:_____

    B. Problem: _____

        1. Solution:_____

    C. Problem: _____

        1. Solution:_____

EXERCISE 5.31

Directions: Write about or discuss the following questions.

Now that you have had some time to adjust to the United States and the educational system here, think about some of the similarities and differences between higher education here and in your country. What aspects of the two systems are similar? Which are different? What areas do you think will be the most difficult to adjust to? Why? How do you plan to go about making some of these adjustments?

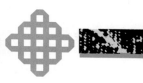

In Chapter 5, you had the chance to put many of the skills that you learned in this course together. If you keep up to date with your work, review your course material frequently, begin to prepare for tests and projects well in advance, and ask for clarification when it is necessary, you can do well in college. If you have a good attitude and plan to be successful, you will be. Good luck in your studies!

ON YOUR OWN	IN CLASS
Working with a Group	
	Understanding the Assignment
Meeting Deadlines	
Choosing a Topic	
Brainstorming	
Writing a Thesis Statement	
Using Books as References	
Writing One-Sentence Summaries	
Knowing Your Audience	
Thinking Critically	
	Arguing Persuasively
Completing the Project	
	Presenting Your Project to the Class
Setting Priorities	
Analyzing Your Academic Strengths and Weaknesses	

Appendix A
Textbook Chapters

COMMUNICATION BETWEEN CULTURES

LARRY A. SAMOVAR
San Diego State University

RICHARD E. PORTER
California State University, Long Beach

Wadsworth Publishing Company
Belmont, California
A Division of Wadsworth, Inc.

Culture is man's medium; there is not one aspect of human life that is not touched and altered by culture. This means personality, how people express themselves (including shows of emotion), the way they think, how they move, how problems are solved, how their cities are planned and laid out, how transportation systems function and are organized, as well as how economic and government systems are put together and function. However, ... it is frequently the most obvious and taken-for-granted and therefore the least studied aspects of culture that influence behavior in the deepest and most subtle ways.

EDWARD T. HALL

People in Paris eat snails, but people in San Diego put poison on them. Why? People in Iran sit on the floor and pray five times each day, but people in Las Vegas sit up all night in front of slot machines. Why? Some people speak Tagalog, others speak English. Why? Some people paint and decorate their entire bodies, but others spend millions of dollars painting and decorating only their faces. Why? Some people talk to God, but others have God talk to them. Why? The general answer to all these questions is the same. People seem to think, feel, believe, and strive for what their culture considers proper. Using the language of the last chapter, people respond to the world in light of the messages they have received, and culture determines the form, pattern, and content of those messages. This omnipresent quality of culture leads Hall to conclude that "there is not one aspect of human life that is not touched and altered by culture."[1] In many ways Hall is correct; culture is everything. And more importantly, at least for the purposes of this book, *culture and communication work in tandem*—they are inseparable. In fact, it is often difficult to decide which is the voice and which is the echo.

Culture dictates who talks to whom, about what, how, when, and for how long. It helps govern the conditions and circumstances under which various messages may or may not be sent, noticed, or interpreted. Our entire repertory of communicative behaviors depends largely on the culture in which we have been raised. Remember, we aren't born knowing how to dress, what toys to play with, what to eat, which gods to worship, or how to spend our money and our time. Culture is both teacher and textbook. From how much eye contact we employ to explanations of why we get sick, culture plays a dominant role in our lives. It is the foundation of communication; and when cultures vary, communication practices may also vary.

Culture and communication are so inextricably bound to one another that some cultural anthropologists (and the authors of this book) believe the terms *culture* and *communication* are essentially synonymous.[2] This relationship between culture and communication is the key factor in understanding communication, and more specifically, intercultural communication. Our ability to recognize the complexities of intercultural communication must begin with a sound grasp of the cultural influences on the way people communicate. To assist you in developing an appropriate perspective for the study of intercultural communication, we plan to do for culture many of the same things we did for communication in the last chapter. We shall explain why cultures develop, define culture, discuss the major ingredients of culture, and isolate the characteristics of culture that most directly relate to communication.

Culture

Throughout Chapter 2 we apologized for reducing a topic as complex as communication to simple terms. We fear that here in Chapter 3 we must revert to that same plea. We are now faced with the task of grappling with a concept that is not only complex but, as we just noted, has the potential to include nearly everything. We shall, however, attack the ubiquitous nature of culture in much the same way we did the all-inclusive character of communication. We plan to look only at those aspects of culture that are most germane to the study of intercultural communication.

THE BASIC FUNCTION OF CULTURE

It is believed that our ancestors evolved culture for much the same reason we have cultures today. Both then and now, culture serves the basic need of laying out a predictable world in which an individual is firmly oriented. Culture enables us to make sense of our surroundings. As Thomas Fuller wrote two hundred years ago, "Culture makes all things easy." Although this view might be slightly overstated, culture does ease the transition from the womb to this new life by giving meaning to events, objects, and people in the environment. In this way culture makes the world a less mysterious place.

From the instant of birth, a child is formally and informally taught how to behave. Common behaviors and definable settings allow for automatic responses that can be forecasted. Children, regardless of the culture, quickly learn how to behave in a manner that is acceptable to adults. Conversely, they are also told that if they are good they will be rewarded. Within each culture, therefore, there is no need to expend energy deciding what each event means or how to respond to it. The assumption is that people who share a common culture can usually be counted on to behave "correctly" and predictably. Hence, culture reduces the chances of surprises by shielding people from the unknown. It offers each of its members a common blueprint for all of life's activities. Try to imagine a single day in your life without having access to the guidelines your culture provides. Without the "rules" that govern your actions, you would soon feel helpless. From how to greet strangers to how to spend our time, culture provides us with structure. To lack culture is to lack structure. Without both we would be intellectually defenseless, floundering animals in an unfathomable realm. We might even go so far as to say that "our primary mode of biological adaptation is culture, not anatomy."[3] Culture teaches each of us how to make the most of what we have gained through millions of years of evolution.

SOME DEFINITIONS OF CULTURE

If culture were a single thing we would need only one definition. We have already indicated, however, that culture, like communication, is ubiquitous, multidimensional, complex, and all-pervasive. Because culture is so broad in its scope, scholars have had a difficult time arriving at one central theory or definition of what it is. As with communication, many definitions have been suggested—perhaps as many as 150 in the literature. These definitions range from those that conceive of culture as an all-encompassing phenomenon ("it is everything"), to those that take a narrower view of the concept ("it is opera, art, and ballet"). Let us examine some of these definitions so that we might better understand the place of culture in intercultural communication.

Hoebel and Frost see culture in nearly all human activity. They define culture as an "integrated system of learned behavior patterns which are characteristic of the members of a society and which are not the result of biological inheritance."[4] For them culture is not genetically predetermined; it is noninstinctive.[5] The reasoning behind this position is twofold. First, people who claim the liberal orientation believe that culture is transmitted and maintained solely through communication and learning.[6] All scholars of culture begin with this same assumption—that is, that culture is learned. It is the second leg of the argument that best identifies scholars who take the sweeping view. These scholars contend that the act of birth confines each individual to a specific geographic location, a location that exposes people to certain messages while at the same time denying them others. All of these messages, whether they be conveyed through a certain language, religion, food, dress, housing, toys, or books, are culturally based; therefore, everything that a person experiences is part of his or her culture.

From a definition that includes all learned behavior we can move to definitions that propose culture has tangible boundaries. But here again scholars have not agreed on the boundaries. Some, such as Triandis, take an expansive view of culture, suggesting that culture "can be distinguished as having both objective (e.g., roads, tools) and subjective (e.g., norms, laws, values) aspects."[7] Those who define culture in this way look at what a culture does to its environment as well as what it does to its people.

Cole and Scribner offer a definition of culture that ties culture to human cognition:

> Perception, memory, and thinking all develop as part of the general socialization of a child and are inseparably bound up with the patterns of activity, communication, and social relations into which he enters. . . . His every experience has been shaped by the culture of which he is a member and is infused with socially defined meanings and emotions.[8]

Hofstede has advanced another definition that views culture from a psychological perspective: "Culture is the collective programming of the mind which distinguishes the members of one category of people from another."[9] Both of these definitions stress the mental conditions that cultural experiences impose. Definitions of culture, like definitions of communication, reflect the specific research emphasis of the person offering the definition. For example, an assessment of culture from a *communication* approach would define culture "as the complex combination of common symbols, knowledge, folklore conventions, language, information-processing patterns, rules, rituals, habits, life styles, and attitudes that link and give a common identity to a particular group of people at a particular point in time."[10]

The lack of agreement on any one definition of culture led anthropologists Kroeber and Kluckhohn to review some five hundred definitions, phrasings, and uses of the concept. From their analysis they proposed the following definition:

> Culture consists of patterns, explicit and implicit, of and for behavior acquired and transmitted by symbols, constituting the distinctive achievements of human groups, including their embodiments in artifacts; the essential core of culture consists of traditional (i.e., historically derived and selected) ideas and especially their attached values; culture systems may, on the one hand, be considered as products of action, and on the other as conditioning elements of further action.[11]

Although we believe that the Kroeber and Kluckhohn definition is broad enough to include most of the major territory of culture, we nevertheless have evolved a definition that we believe is most suited to the goals of this book. We define **culture** *as the deposit of knowledge, experience, beliefs, values, attitudes, meanings, hierarchies, religion, notions of time, roles, spatial relations, concepts of the universe, and material objects and possessions acquired by a group of people in the course of generations through individual and group striving.*

THE INGREDIENTS OF CULTURE

Our review of definitions of culture should have made it clear that culture is composed of many ingredients. It might be helpful to look at some of these ingredients, and their subcomponents as a way of understanding the composition of culture.

The ingredients of culture, like the definitions, often seem at variance with one another. Most scholars agree, however, that any description should include the three aspects submitted by Almaney and Alwan, who contend that

cultures may be classified by three large categories of elements: artifacts (which include items ranging from arrowheads to hydrogen bombs, magic charms to antibiotics, torches to electric lights, and chariots to jet planes); concepts (which include such beliefs or value systems as right or wrong, God and man, ethics, and the general meaning of life); and behaviors (which refer to the actual practice of concepts or beliefs.[12]

The authors then provide an excellent example of how these three aspects might be reflected within a culture: "Whereas money is considered an artifact, the value placed upon it is a concept, but the actual spending and saving of money is behavior."[13]

Other inventories usually add to or further partition the three ingredients Almaney and Alwan describe. According to Cateora and Hess, culture is comprised of the following elements:

- Material culture (technology, economics)
- Social institutions (social organizations, political structures)
- Individuals and the universe (belief systems)
- Aesthetics (graphics, plastic arts, folklore, music, drama, dance)
- Language[14]

It should be evident that the word *culture* as well as the reality of culture is complex and multidimensional. It can include everything from rites of passage to concepts of the soul. Think for just a moment of all the beliefs you hold and the objects that have meaning for you because you are a member of one culture or another. Your views of work, dress, etiquette, healing and health, death, play, hygiene, superstition, modesty, sex, status, courtship, and the like are part of your cultural membership.

In Chapter 2 we observed some major problems associated with isolating specific elements for any complex activity. Some of these lessons are worth remembering when we examine the ingredients of culture. First, we asserted that any single listing of ingredients would be incomplete; and second, that the items selected would reflect the point of view of the person preparing the list. These same two qualifications apply to the composition of such a list for culture. For example, the ingredients we have examined so far are general enough to be included in any analysis of culture. However, if we were to move to particular orientations towards the study of culture, we would begin to encounter modifications. Two instances will serve to illustrate this point, one that links culture and international business, and another that links culture to human communication.

Terpstra maintains that any analysis of culture in the *business context* must embrace eight major elements and an array of specific factors. Notice as we list some of these factors how they mirror the business arena:

- Language (spoken, written, official, hierarchical, international, and so on)
- Religion (sacred objects, philosophical systems, beliefs and norms, prayer, taboos, holidays, rituals)
- Values and attitudes (toward time, achievement, work, wealth, change, scientific method, risk-taking)
- Education (formal education, vocational training, higher education, literacy level, human resources planning)
- Social organization (kinship, social institutions, authority structures, interest groups, social mobility and stratification)
- Technology and material culture (transportation, energy systems, tools, science, invention)
- Politics (nationalism, imperialism, power, national interests, ideologies, political risk)
- Law (common law, foreign law, international law, antitrust policy, regulations)[15]

As we offer our second list of cultural ingredients, notice once again how they reflect the perspective of the list maker—in this case someone interested in communication and culture. Dodd identifies the following fourteen elements as common to all cultures: cultural history, cultural personality, material culture, role relationships, art, language, cultural stability, cultural beliefs, ethnocentrism, nonverbal behavior, spatial relations, time, recognition and reward, and thought patterns.[16]

Keep in mind that what Terpstra did for business and culture, and Dodd for communication and culture, others have done with education, health care, and the like. They all end up isolating those aspects of culture that are reflected in the area with which they are most concerned. We, too, shall select parts of culture when we advance our personal inventory.

As we leave this section on the ingredients of culture, we would like you to keep a few things in mind. First, several of the lists we presented contained some of the same items. This is because regardless of the researcher, there is a common core of elements. Second, once scholars list the established elements, they select those portions of culture that most represent their areas of interest. Third, any slate of elements is bound to be insufficient. There are so many elements of culture that one proposal or theory could never contain them all. Finally, although the elements can be found in every culture, the emphasis and manifestation of each element are culturally based. That is to say, all cultures have a language, for example, but each has its own special language.

Having discussed the roots of culture, some of its definitions and ingredients, we are now ready to focus on those aspects of culture that one must understand in order to communicate successfully with someone from a different background.

THE CHARACTERISTICS OF CULTURE

Culture is not innate; it is learned. We begin with the single most important characteristic of culture, and the one that is hardest to explain. It is the most important because it goes to the heart of what is called culture. It is the most difficult to explain because we must ask the word *learned* to stand for more than one thing. Let's use these two notions as the vehicle to clarify this first characteristic.

Without the advantages of learning from those who lived before us we would not have culture. Babies cut off from all adult care, training, and supervision would instinctively eat, drink, defecate, urinate, gurgle, and cry. But what they would eat, when they would eat, where they would defecate, and the like would be random. Without learning, they would "communicate" even emotional states with gestures and sounds—not language as we know it. Children without information about the past would not have utensils, arts, religion, government, courtship behaviors, and all the other traits that make us human. They would evolve some kind of social order, but one void of a history that could be communicated; they would not be like any other culture. For as we mentioned previously, culture is the collection of life patterns that our elders give us. And while some knowledge conceivably is genetically transmitted, most of our behavior patterns must be learned. As we implied in the title of this chapter, culture is both teacher and subject matter.

Our second introductory assertion regarding the word *learning is* somewhat more enigmatic than our first. The problem is that we all behave as if a word stood for only one thing—and of course there are times when it does. A single word, however, often must stand for many things. Think for a moment of the word *pain*. How different the meaning can be when the word denotes the discomfort from a small splinter in the finger versus the anguish of a burn victim. When we look at the word *learned* as it applies to culture, we find the same problem, for in the context of culture the word has numerous meanings. That is to say, we learn our culture in many different ways. The little boy in North America whose father tells him to shake hands when he is introduced to a friend of the family is learning culture. The Arab baby who is read the Koran when he or she is one day old is learning culture. The Indian child who lives in a home where the women eat after the men is learning culture. The Jewish child who helps conduct the Passover celebration is learning culture.

The term **enculturation** denotes this total activity of learning one's culture. More specifically, enculturation is "conscious or unconscious conditioning occurring within that process whereby the individual, as child and adult, achieves competence in a particular culture."[17] Enculturation usually takes place through *interaction* (your parents kiss you and you learn about kissing—whom to kiss, when to kiss, and so on), *observation* (you watch your father do most of the driving of the family car and you learn about sex roles—what a man does, what a woman does), and *imitation* (you laugh at the same jokes your parents laugh at and you learn about humor—it is funny if someone falls down but doesn't get hurt).

In social psychology and sociology the term **socialization** is often used synonymously with *enculturation*. Regardless of which word is applied, the idea remains the same. From infancy on, members of a culture learn their patterns of behavior and ways of thinking until they become internalized. The power and influence of these behaviors and perceptions can be seen in the ways in which we acquire culture. Our learning through interaction, observation, and imitation can take many forms. The concept is best understood by remembering the words conscious and unconscious used in the definition we just offered. These two words help explain the broad and sweeping definition of learning we referred to earlier.

Conscious learning is the easier to see and to explain. In its simplest form it involves the ingredients of our culture that we were told about or that we read about. We learned them at the conscious level. A mother tells her young son to take a bath before he goes to bed, and he learns health habits and cleanliness. A father tells his daughter to say "thank you" when someone pays her a compliment, and she is learning. A grandmother tells her grandchild how to play with certain toys, and the child is learning. A young girl reads the rules for bicycle safety, and she is learning. A teacher tells a pupil the correct way to sit in class, and the pupil is learning. In each of these instances (and there are many others), the person is told what to learn. However, it is at the second level of learning, the unconscious level, that we learn the bulk of what we call culture.

Since culture influences us from the very day we are born, we are rarely conscious of many of the messages that we are receiving. This "hidden dimension" of culture leads many researchers to claim that culture is invisible. Ruben, for example, writes that "the presence of culture is so subtle and pervasive that it simply goes unnoticed. It's there now, it's been there as long as anyone can remember, and few of us have reason to think much about it."[18] Most of us would have a difficult time pointing to a specific event or experience that taught us about such things as direct eye contact, our use of silence and space, the importance of attractiveness, our view of aging, our ability to speak one language over another, our preference for activity over meditation, and countless other behaviors that are unique to our particular culture. In all of these cases we were learning the perceptions, rules, and behaviors of membership without being aware of it.

Although learned on the unconscious level, the significant perceptions, rules, and behaviors are given added strength by the fact that members of any culture receive ongoing reinforcement for those aspects of culture that are deemed most crucial. For example, in North America the importance of being thin is repeated with such regularity that we all take this value for granted. In addition, the messages that are strategic for any culture come from a variety of sources. That is to say, parents, schools, plays, folktales, music, art, church, the media, and peers all repeat those assumptions on which any culture operates. Think for a moment of the thousands of ways you have been "told" the importance of being popular and well-liked, or the many messages you have received concerning competition and winning. Our games, sports, toys, movies, and so on all tell us about the need to win. A famous tennis player tells us that he "feels like dying when he comes in second." And the president of a major car company concludes his television pitch by announcing, "We want to be number one—what else is there?"

Although the "carriers" of culture are nearly the same for all of us (parents, peers, church, and so on), the messages they transmit reflect the character of each culture. A case in point is the popular folktale "Cinderella. " Although nearly every culture has a version, each culture uses the tale to emphasize a value that is important to that particular culture. For example, the North American version stresses Cinderella's attractiveness as a reflection of her inner qualities. She is also, however, rather passive and weak. In the Algonquin Indian tale the virtues of truthfulness and intellectual honesty are the basis for the Cinderella character. The Japanese story accents the value of intellectual ability and gentleness. In one version there are only two sisters who wish to go to the Kabuki theater. In place of the famous "slipper test" is the challenge of having to compose a song extemporaneously. One sister manages only a simple unimaginative song, which she sings in a loud voice. But Cinderella composes a song that has both meter and metaphor, and she sings it in soft tones. She, of course, is shown to deserve the rewards of such actions. This rather long example shows that the lessons of culture may travel by similar channels—in this case folktales—but they contain different patterns and values.

We conclude our description of this initial characteristic of culture by reminding you of how our discussion directly relates to intercultural communication. First, many of the behaviors we label as cultural are not only automatic and invisible; we often produce them without being aware of our action. For example, in North American culture women smile more than men. Yet they "learned" that behavior below the level of consciousness and perform it almost habitually. Hence, such cultural behavior tends to be unconscious in both its acquisition and expression.

Our second point is a theme we have repeated throughout this chapter: Common experiences produce common behaviors. The sharing of experience and behaviors is what makes a culture unique. Put in slightly different language, culture separates one group of people from another. This separation, and how to understand it, is what this book is all about.

Culture is transmissible from person to person, group to group, and generation to generation.   Much of our discussion to this point has indicated the strong link between culture and communication. This new characteristic—that culture is transmissible—simply adds credence to that position. It also points out that the symbols of a culture are what enable us to pass on the content and patterns of a culture. We can use the spoken word as a symbol and tell others about the importance of freedom. We can use the written word as a symbol and let others read about "the War of Independence." We can use nonverbal actions as symbols and show others that we usually shake hands to greet one another. We can use flags as symbols to claim territory or demonstrate loyalty. We can use automobiles or jewelry as symbols to show others about success and status. We can use a cross to show our love of God. As you would suspect, the use of symbols is at the core of culture. Other animals are limited in their use of symbols and therefore are incapable of developing a culture.

The portability of symbols allows us to package and store them as well as transmit them. The mind, books, pictures, films, videos, and the like enable a culture to preserve what it deems to be important and worthy of transmission. Hence, each individual, regardless of his or her generation, is heir to a massive "library" of information that has been collected in anticipation of his or her entry into the culture. In this sense, culture is historical as well as preservable. Each new generation might write more, but the notes from the past represent what we call culture. As Proust wrote, "The past remains the present."

It is important for any student of intercultural communication to remember that many of the behaviors a culture selects to pass on are universal. However, because culture, like communication, is subjective, there are also countless messages that are unique to each culture. Americans tell each generation to value individualism. In Japan the message is that the group comes before the individual. North Americans tell each generation that competition is valuable. For Mexicans and Native Americans the message is that cooperation is more important than the contest. North Americans tell each generation to value youth. In China the message is to respect and treasure the elderly. Each of these examples makes the same point: *The content of culture is subjective and communicable.*

As we noted earlier, one thing that makes the transferring of culture from generation to generation so interesting is that much of the movement is invisible and unconscious. Jews, to this day, while reading from the Torah, sway backwards and forwards like camel-riders. They have "inherited" this simple act unconsciously from centuries ago, when Jews were prohibited from riding camels. The pretense of riding was developed as a form of compensation. Although the motive for the action is gone, the action gets passed on to each new generation by means of what Hall calls the "silent language" of culture.

Culture is a dynamic system that changes continuously over time. This current characteristic is yet another example of how communication and culture are alike. For you will recall that in the last chapter we highlighted that communication was not static, but rather was a dynamic, constantly changing process. We now suggest that cultures are also subject to fluctuations, that they seldom remain constant. As ideas and products evolve within a culture, they can produce change. Although cultures change through several mechanisms, the three most common are invention, diffusion, and calamity.

Invention is usually defined as the discovery of new practices, tools, or concepts that most members of the culture eventually accept. In North America the Civil Right's Movement and the invention of television are two good examples of how ideas and products reshape a culture.

Diffusion, or borrowing from another culture, is another way in which change occurs. The assimilation of what is borrowed accelerates as cultures come into direct contact with each other. For example, as Japan and North America have more commerce, we see Americans assimilating Japanese business practices and the Japanese using American marketing tactics.

Although invention and diffusion are the most common causes of change, there are of course other factors that foster shifts in a culture. The concept of **cultural calamity** illustrates how cultures change. Reflect for a moment on how the calamity of the Vietnam War has brought changes to both Vietnam and the United States. Not only did it create a new population of refugees, but it also forced us to reevaluate some cultural assumptions concerning global influence and military power.

From the preceding discussion it should be clear that cultures are very adaptive. History runs over with examples of how cultures have been forced to alter their course because of natural disasters, wars, or other calamities. Events in the last few hundred years have scattered Jews throughout the world, yet their culture has adapted and survived. And think for a moment about the adaptiveness of the Japanese. Their government and economy were nearly destroyed during World War II, yet because they could adapt, their culture endured and they are now a major economic force in the world.

We would be remiss if we failed to indicate that although many aspects of culture are subject to change, the deep structure of a culture resists major alterations. That is to say, changes in dress, food, transportation, housing, and the like, though appearing to be important, are simply attached to the existing value system. However, values associated with such things as ethics and morals, work and leisure, definitions of freedom, the importance of the past, religious practices, the pace of life, and attitudes towards gender and age are so very deep in a culture that they persist generation after generation. Even demands for a more liberal government in countries such as China and the Soviet Union have their roots in the history of those countries. In the United States, studies conducted on American values show that most of the central values of the 1980s are similar to the values of the last two hundred years. In short, when analyzing the degree of change within a culture, you must always consider what it is that is changing. Don't be fooled because downtown Tokyo looks much like Paris or New York. Most of what we call culture is below the surface. It is like the moon—we observe the front, which is flat and one-dimensional, but there is another side and dimensions that we cannot see.

Culture is selective. Every culture represents a limited choice of behavior patterns from the total of human experience. This selection, whether it be what shoes to wear or how to reach God, is made according to the basic assumptions and values that are meaningful to each culture. Because each individual has only these limited experiences, what we know is but an abstraction of what there is to know. Put in slightly different terms, culture defines the boundaries of different groups.[19]

This characteristic is important to all students of intercultural communication for two reasons. First, it is a reminder that what a culture selects to tell each generation is a reflection of what that culture deems important. In the United States, for example, being healthy is highly valued, and therefore messages related to that idea are isolated. Second, the notion of selectivity also suggests that cultures tend to separate one group from another. If one culture stresses (selects) work as an end (Japan), while another emphasizes work as a means to an end (Mexico), we tend to have a separation.

The various facets of culture are interrelated. This characteristic serves to underscore the complex nature of culture. Hall clearly states the meaning of this sentence when he writes, "You touch a culture in one place and everything else is affected."[20] A good example of this characteristic is the Women's Movement in the United States. Although the phrase is made up of only two words, the phenomenon has been like a large stone cast into a pond. The Women's Movement has brought about changes in sexual practices, educational opportunities, the legal system, career opportunities, and even male-female interaction. Hence, this one aspect of culture has actually altered other patterns and values.

Many mass-communication experts believe that this interconnectedness of culture is at the core of the "cultural imperialism" hypothesis. This hypothesis maintains that by broadcasting American programs to Third World countries, for example, we are actually making them like us. The argument is that if we send programs that glorify material possessions to a culture that stresses spiritual life, we are touching many aspects of their culture. Or put another way, if you interfere with one facet of a culture you alter other facets.

Culture is ethnocentric. The disposition towards ethnocentrism (centeredness on one's own group) might well be the characteristic that most directly relates to intercultural communication. The important tie between ethnocentrism and communication can be seen in the definition of the word itself. Keesing notes that ethnocentrism is "a universal tendency for any people to put its own culture and society in a central position of priority and worth."[21] In other words, ethnocentrism becomes the perceptual prism through which cultures interpret and judge all other groups. These interpretations and judgements include everything from what the "out-groups" value to how they communicate. In this sense ethnocentrism leads to a subjective evaluation of how another culture conducts its daily business. That this evaluation can only be negative is clear if you realize that a logical extension of ethnocentrism is the position that "our way is the right way." Most discussions of ethnocentrism even enlarge the concept to include feelings of superiority. As Keesing writes, "Nearly always the folklore of a people includes myths of origin which give priority to themselves, and place the stamp of supernatural approval upon their particular customs." [22]

As we have pointed out, feelings that "we are right" and "they are wrong" cover every aspect of a culture's existence. Examples range from the insignificant ("earrings should be placed on the ears, not on the nose") to the significant ("we need to fight and die for what is right"). When these kinds of attitudes are carried to their extreme, as they often are, ethnocentrism can be a major hindrance to intercultural understanding. The logical extension of ethnocentrism is detachment and division, which can take a variety of forms, including the severance of co-cultures from the dominant culture, or one major culture avoiding another. How often we see examples of white-collar workers isolated from blue-collar workers, blacks living apart from whites, and those with disabilities removed from our sight. And on an international level, we observe East Indians looking down on the Pakistanis, the Japanese feeling superior to the Chinese, Mexicans unconsciously sequestering their Indian population, and Americans not trusting the Russians.

Our discussion thus far should not lead to the conclusion that ethnocentrism is always intentional, for much of it is not. Like culture itself, ethnocentrism is usually learned at the unconscious level, while we are actually learning something else. If, for example, our schools are teaching American history, geography, literature, and government, they are also, without realizing it, teaching ethnocentrism. For the student, by being exposed only to this single orientation, is developing the view that America is the center of the world, as well as learning to judge that world by North American standards—the standards he or she has been taught. If most of the authors, philosophers, scientists, composers, and political leaders you have learned about are white males, you will use white males to judge other cultures.

What makes the pull of culture so very strong, as we indicated earlier in the chapter, is that the "teaching" begins at birth and continues all through life. Although the language she uses to make this important point is sexist by today's standards, Ruth Benedict nevertheless has offered an excellent explanation of why culture is such a powerful force.

> The life history of the individual is first and foremost an accommodation to the patterns and standards traditionally handed down in his community. From the moment of his birth the customs into which he is born shape his experience and behavior. By the time he can talk, he is the little creature of his culture, and by the time he is grown and able to take part in its activities, its habits are his habits, its beliefs his beliefs, its impossibilities his impossibilities. Every child that is born into his group will share them with him, and no child born into the opposite side of the globe can ever achieve the thousandth part. [23]

Regardless of who or what is the culprit, ethnocentrism can impede intercultural interaction. We shall therefore return to this topic throughout this volume as we offer advice for improving the way you communicate with people from different cultures.

Summary

CULTURE

- The basic function of culture is to explain the world to each new inhabitant of the culture. The world is a confusing place until we can make some sense of it. Culture, by telling us what to expect, reduces confusion and helps us predict the future.
- We define culture as the deposit of knowledge, experience, beliefs, values, attitudes, meanings, hierarchies, religion, timing, roles, spatial relationships, concepts of the universe, and material objects acquired by a group of people in the course of generations through individual and group striving.
- Culture has many ingredients, such as food preferences, notions of death, housing requirements, and attitudes towards aging.
- Six characteristics of culture that most directly affect communication are that it is (1) learned, (2) transmissible, (3) dynamic, (4) selective, (5) composed of interrelated facets, and (6) ethnocentric.

Activities

1. Ask your informant to relate a folktale (or a song, a work of art, or something else appropriate) from his or her culture. What cultural values does it convey? Compare your informant's folktale to one from your culture. Does it stand in opposition to yours, or are there similarities?
2. In small groups, list the North American cultural values mentioned in this chapter (there are several). Add any others you can think of. Then find examples from North American advertising campaigns that reveal these values. An example is an advertising slogan from an athletic shoe manufacturer, "Just do it, " which reflects the North American value of activity.

Discussion Ideas

1. Explain North American views toward these elements of culture: work, dress, hygiene, courtship, sex, and status.
2. Describe a typical day from morning to night in terms of the cultural "rules" that govern your actions. Indicate what you've been trained to do and what you think the cultural "rule" is. For example:

ACTION	RULE
Brush teeth; take shower	Personal odors are offensive in N. American culture
Put on jeans and T-shirt	Comfort and informality are acceptable in educational settings

3. Give additional examples, from recent history, of cultures that have undergone changes through invention, diffusion, and calamity.

4. There are now several fast-food restaurants (such as McDonald's) in France. Does this mean that traditional French values regarding food and eating have changed? Explain your answer.

Notes for Chapter 3

1. Edward T. Hall, *Beyond Culture* (Garden City, NY: Anchor, Doubleday, 1977), 14.

2. See Alfred G. Smith, ed., *Communication and Culture: Readings in the Codes of Human Interaction* (New York: Holt, Rinehart, and Winston, 1966), 1–14; Edward T. Hall, *The Silent Language* (Greenwich, CT: Fawcett, 1959); *The Hidden Dimension* (Garden City, NY: Doubleday, 1966); *Beyond Culture* (New York: Anchor Press/Doubleday, 1977).

3. Marvin Harris, *Cows, Pigs, Wars, and Witches: The Riddles of Culture* (New York: Random House, 1974), 84.

4. E. Adamson Hoebel and Everett L. Frost, *Cultural and Social Anthropology* (New York: McGraw-Hill, 1976), 6.

5. Hoebel and Frost.

6. Hoebel and Frost.

7. Harry C. Triandis, "A Theoretical Framework for the More Efficient Construction of Culture Assimilators," *International Journal of Intercultural Relations* 8 (1984), 305.

8. Michael Cole and Sylvia Scribner, *Culture and Thought: A Psychological Introduction* (New York: Wiley, 1974), 8.

9. Geert Hofstede, "National Cultures and Corporate Cultures" (Paper delivered on LIFIM Perspective Day, Helsinki, Finland, December 4, 1984).

10. Brent D. Ruben, *Communication and Human Behavior,* 2d ed. (New York: Macmillan, 1988), 384.

11. A. L. Kroeber and Clyde Kluckhohn, "Culture: A Critical Review of Concepts and Definitions," *Harvard University Peabody Museum of American Archeology and Ethnology Papers* 47 (1952), 181.

12. A. J. Almaney and A. J. Alwan, *Communicating with the Arabs* (Prospect Heights, IL: Waveland Press, 1982), 5.

13. Almaney and Alwan, 5.

14. Philip Cateora and John Hess, *International Marketing* (Homewood, IL: Irwin, 1979), 89.

15. Vern Terpstra, *The Cultural Environment of International Business* (Cincinnati: South-Western, 1978), xiv.

16. Carley H. Dodd, *Dynamics of Intercultural Communication,* 2d ed. (Dubuque, IA: Wm. C. Brown, 1987), 40-49.

17. Hoebel and Frost, 58.

18. Ruben, 396.

19. Hall, 13-14.

20. Hall.

21. Felix M. Keesing, *Cultural Anthropology: The Science of Custom* (New York: Holt, Rinehart, and Winston, 1965), 46.

22. Keesing.

23. Ruth Benedict, *Patterns of Culture* (New York: Mentor Books, 1948), 2.

Media/Impact

An Introduction to Mass Media

Second Edition

Shirley Biagi
California State University, Sacramento

Wadsworth Publishing Company/Belmont, California/A Division of Wadsworth, Inc.

To understand the mass media, first it is important to understand the process of communication. Communication is the act of sending ideas and attitudes from one person to another. Writing and talking to each other are only two ways human beings communicate. We also communicate when we gesture, move our bodies, or roll our eyes.

Three terms that scholars use to describe how people communicate are *intrapersonal communication, interpersonal communication,* and *mass communication.* Each communication situation involves different numbers of people in specific ways.

If you are in a grocery store and you silently discuss with yourself whether to buy a package of chocolate chip cookies, you are using what scholars call *intrapersonal communication:* communication within one person.

To communicate with each other, people use many of the five senses—sight, hearing, touch, smell, and taste. Scholars call this direct sharing of experience between two people *interpersonal communication.*

1.1

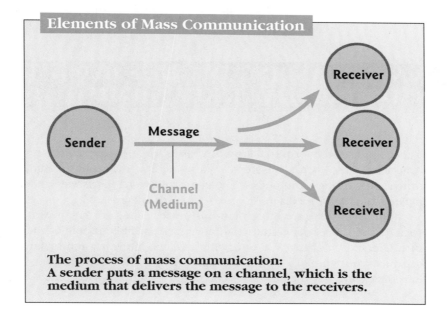

Elements of Mass Communication

**The process of mass communication:
A sender puts a message on a channel, which is the medium that delivers the message to the receivers.**

Mass communication is communication from one person or group of persons through a transmitting device (a **medium**) to large audiences or markets. In MEDIA/IMPACT you will study mass communication. (The plural of the word *medium* is *media,* so when scholars discuss more than one medium they refer to media.)

To describe the process of **mass communication,** scholars draw charts and diagrams to convey what happens when people send messages to one another. This description begins with four easily understood terms: *sender, message, receiver,* and *channel* (Figure 1.1).

Pretend that you're standing directly in front of someone and you say, "I like your hat." In this simple communication, you are the sender, the message is "I like your hat," and the person in front of you is the receiver (or audience). This example of interpersonal communication involves the sender, the message, and the receiver.

In mass communication, the sender puts the message on what is called a **channel.** This channel is the medium that delivers the message. A medium is the means by which a message reaches an audience. Radio is the medium that delivers music, for example; television delivers entertainment shows, and newspapers deliver news stories. The radio, television, and newspaper media are simply delivery systems for the messages they carry.

Using a very general definition, mass communication today shares three characteristics:

1. *A message is sent out using some form of mass media (such as newspapers or television).*
2. *The message is delivered rapidly.*
3. *The message reaches large groups of different kinds of people simultaneously or within a short period of time.*

Thus, a telephone conversation between two people would not qualify as mass communication, but a message from the president of the United States, broadcast simultaneously by all the television networks, would qualify.

Mass media deliver messages to large numbers of people at once. The businesses that produce the mass media in America—newspapers, magazines, radio, television, movies, recordings, and books—are mass media industries.

UNDERSTANDING THE MASS MEDIA INDUSTRIES: FOUR KEY THEMES

This book uses the term **mass media industries** to describe the seven types of American mass media businesses: newspapers, magazines, radio, television, movies, recordings, and books. The use of the word *industries* underscores the major goal of mass media in America—financial success.

But the media are more than businesses: They are key institutions in our society. They affect our culture, our buying habits, and our politics, and they are in turn affected by changes in our beliefs, tastes, interests, and behavior. To help organize your thinking about the mass media and their impact, this section introduces four key themes that will recur in the chapters to come.

1. The Media as Businesses

What you see, read, and hear in the American mass media may cajole, entertain, inform, persuade, provoke, and even perplex you. But to understand the American media, the first concept to understand is that the central force driving the media in America is the desire to make money: *American media are businesses, vast businesses.* The products of these businesses are information and entertainment.

Other motives shape the media in America, of course: the desire to fulfill the public's need for information, to influence the country's governance, to disseminate the country's culture, to offer entertainment, and to provide an outlet for artistic expression. But American media are, above all, profit centered (see Impact/Perspective, The Business of Media).

Who Owns the Media? To understand the media, it is important to know who owns these important channels of communication. In America, all of the media are privately owned except the Public Broadcasting Service and National Public Radio, which survive on government support and private donations. The annual budget for public broadcasting, however, is less than 3 percent of the amount of money advertisers pay every year to support America's commercial media.

Many family-owned media properties still exist in the United States, but today the trend in the media industries, like other American industries, is for media companies to cluster together in groups. The top ten newspaper chains, for example, own one-fifth of the nation's daily newspapers. This trend is called **concentration of ownership,** and this concentration takes five different forms.

1. Chains. Benjamin Franklin established America's first newspaper chain. This tradition was expanded by William Randolph Hearst in the 1930s. At their peak, Hearst newspapers accounted for nearly 14 percent of total national daily circulation and nearly 25 percent of Sunday circulation. Today's newspaper chain giant is Gannett, with 82 daily newspapers, including *USA Today.*

Broadcast companies also own chains of stations, but the Federal Communications Commission (FCC) regulates broadcast ownership. Today one company can own no more than 12 TV stations, 12 AM radio stations, and 12 FM radio stations, as long as the total number of stations doesn't reach more than 25 percent of the national audience.

2. Networks. The four major networks are ABC (American Broadcasting Company), NBC (National Broadcasting Company), CBS (Columbia Broadcasting System), and Fox Broadcasting. Beginning with NBC in the 1920s, the three original networks (NBC, CBS, and ABC) were established to deliver radio programming across the country, and the network concept continued with the invention of television. Networks can have as many affiliates as they want, but no network can have two **affiliates** in the same broadcast area. (Affiliates are stations that use network programming but are owned by companies other than the networks.)

Fox is the youngest network, founded in 1986, and serves only television.

3. Cross-Media Ownership. Many media companies own more than one type of media property: newspapers, magazines, radio and TV stations, for example. Gannett, which owns the largest chain of newspapers, also owns television and radio stations. Among the properties of Capital Cities/ABC are the *Kansas City Star, Modern Photography* magazine, San Francisco's KGO radio, KGO-TV, and the ABC network. Rupert Murdoch's News Corporation owns newspapers, television stations, magazines, Twentieth Century-Fox Film, Fox Broadcasting, and HarperCollins Publishers.

4. Conglomerates. When you go to the movies to watch a Columbia picture, you might not realize that Sony owns the film company. Sony is a *conglomerate*— a company that owns media companies as well as companies unrelated to the media business. Media properties can be attractive investments, but some conglomerate owners are unfamiliar with the idiosyncrasies of the media industries.

5. Vertical Integration. The most noticeable trend among today's media companies is **vertical integration**—an attempt to control several related aspects of the media business at once, each part helping the other (see Impact/ Profiles, Four Moguls of the Media). Besides publishing magazines and books, Time Warner, for example, owns Home Box Office (HBO), Warner movie studios, and various cable TV systems throughout the United States. The Japanese company Matsushita owns MCA Records, Universal Studios, and manufactures broadcast production equipment. Paramount Communications owns TV stations, movie theaters, and cable networks as well as the book publishing company Simon & Schuster.

To describe the financial status of today's media is also to talk about acquisitions. The media are buying and selling each other in unprecedented numbers and forming media groups to position themselves in the marketplace to maintain and increase their profits. In 1986, the first time a broadcast network had been sold, *two* networks were sold that year—ABC and NBC. In 1990, 1,080 radio and television properties worth nearly $2 billion changed owners.

Media acquisitions have skyrocketed since 1980 for two reasons. The first is that most conglomerates today are publicly traded companies, which means that their stock is traded on one of the nation's stock exchanges. This makes acquisitions relatively easy.

A media company that wants to buy a publicly owned company can buy that company's stock when the stock becomes available. The open availability of stock in these companies means that anybody with enough money can invest in the American media industries, which is exactly how CBS Board Chairman Laurence Tisch joined the media business (see page 14).

The second reason for the large increase in media alliances is that beginning in 1980, the Federal Communications Commission, under the Reagan administration, gradually deregulated the broadcast media. Before 1980, for example, the FCC allowed one company to own only five TV stations, five AM radio stations, and five FM radio stations.

Companies also were required to hold onto a station for three years before the station could be sold, and the FCC approval process for sales was very complicated. The post-1980 FCC eliminated the three-year rule and raised the number of broadcast holdings allowed for one owner.

The issue of concentrated media ownership is important because some critics fear that concentration means control. That is, if only a few corporations are able to direct the media industries in this country, does this limit the outlets for differing political viewpoints and innovative ideas? (See Impact/Perspective, The Effects of Media Alliances.)

Who Pays for the Mass Media?   Most of the $134 billion a year in income that the American mass media industries collect comes directly from advertisers. Advertising directly supports newspapers, radio, and television. (Subscribers pay only a small part of the cost of producing a newspaper.) Magazines receive more than half of their income from advertising and the other portion from subscriptions. Income for movies, recordings, and books, of course, comes from direct purchases and ticket sales.

This means that most of the information and entertainment you receive from television, radio, newspapers, and magazines in America is paid for by people who want to sell you products. You support the media industries *indirectly* by buying the products that advertisers sell.

Advertising pays most of the bills. One full-page black-and-white ad in *The Wall Street Journal,* for example, costs $105,000. To place a full-page color ad in *Rolling Stone* magazine costs $43,000. A 30-second television commercial in prime time (8 P.M. to 11 P.M.) costs $120,000. Multiply the prices for all these ads in all the media, and you can understand how easily American media industries accumulate the more than $134 billion they collect annually.

You also pay for the media *directly* when you buy a book or a compact disc or go to a movie. This money buys equipment, underwrites company research and expansion, and pays stock dividends. Advertisers and consumers are the financial foundation for American media industries (see Figure 1.2).

1.2

Who Pays for the Media?		
	1990 Spending Shares	
Industry Category	**Advertisers**	**Users**
Newspapers	79%	21%
Magazines	55%	45%
Radio	100%	0%
Television	100%	0%
Cable television	12%	88%
Filmed entertainment	4%	96%
Recordings	0%	100%
Books	0%	100%

SOURCE: Data from *The Veronis, Subler & Associates Communications Industry Forecast,* June 1991, p. 38.

This income also pays salaries to employees. More than 1.5 million people work in the media industries, according to the U.S. Department of Commerce. This number includes all of the people on the payrolls of media companies: reporters, news directors, book editors, magazine art directors, movie producers, and advertising salespeople, for example.

How Does Each Media Industry Work?   Books, newspapers, and magazines were America's only mass media for 250 years after the first American book was published in 1640. The first half of the 20th century brought four new media—movies, radio, recordings, and television—in less than 50 years.

To understand how this happened and where each medium fits in the mass media industries today, it is important to examine the individual characteristics of each medium. (For a comparison of income and employment in the media industries, see Figure 1.3.)

Newspapers. There are about 1,600 daily newspapers in the United States. Evening papers outnumber morning papers 3 to 1, but the number of evening papers is declining. Papers that come out in the morning are growing in circulation, and papers that come out in the afternoon are shrinking. The number of weekly newspapers is also declining—from 8,714 in 1960 to about 7,550 in 1990. Advertising makes up about two-thirds of the printed space in daily newspapers. Newspaper income is expected to remain steady over the next decade, with very little growth.

Magazines. According to the Magazine Publishers Association, about 12,000 magazines are published in the United States. This number is remaining steady. To maintain and increase profits, magazines are raising their subscription and single-copy prices and fighting to maintain their advertising income. The number of magazines people buy by subscription is going up, but newsstand sales are going down. Magazine income is expected to decline slightly in the next decade.

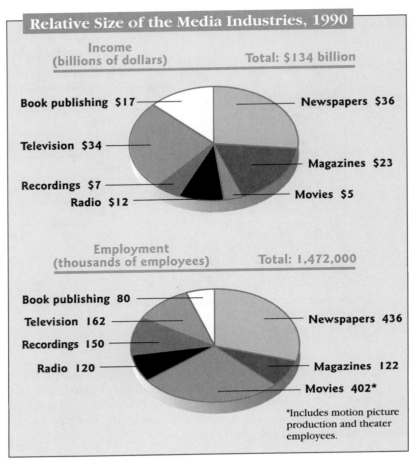

Relative Size of the Media Industries, 1990

Income
(billions of dollars)   Total: $134 billion

Book publishing $17
Television $34
Recordings $7
Radio $12

Newspapers $36
Magazines $23
Movies $5

Employment
(thousands of employees)   Total: 1,472,000

Book publishing 80
Television 162
Recordings 150
Radio 120

Newspapers 436
Magazines 122
Movies 402*

*Includes motion picture
production and theater
employees.

SOURCE: Data from *U.S. Industrial Outlook*, 1991; Bureau of Labor Statistics;
Variety; Federal Communications Commission.

Radio. More than 12,000 radio stations broadcast programming in the United States, about evenly divided between AM and FM. About 1,700 of these stations are noncommercial, most of them FM. The average American household owns five radios. Radio revenues are expected to grow slightly in the next decade.

Television. About 1,400 television stations are operating in the United States; one out of four stations is noncommercial. Many of the stations are affiliated with one of the four major networks—NBC, CBS, ABC, or Fox—although an increasing number of stations, called *independents,* are not affiliated with any network.

Ted Turner launched Cable News Network (CNN) in 1980 to serve cable companies. More than half the homes in the United States are wired for cable, and half the nation's viewers receive 33 or more channels. Cable receives about 7 percent of the overall money spent on television advertising. Network income is declining, while income to independents and cable operators is going up. Total industry revenue is projected to grow at about 7 percent a year.

Movies. Nearly 24,000 theater screens exist in the United States. Only 900 of them are drive-ins. The major and independent studios combined make

How People Spend Their Media Dollars

Per-person spending per year in the United States

Medium	1990	1985	% change
Cable television	$71.73	$42.44	+69%
Books	$64.46	$45.33	+42%
Home video	$59.64	$15.16	+293%
Newspapers	$50.37	$45.33	+11%
Recordings	$41.26	$25.10	+64%
Magazines	$41.04	$29.84	+38%
Movies	$27.48	$21.44	+28%
TOTAL	$355.98	$244.64	+58%

SOURCE: Data from *The Veronis, Subler & Associates Communications Industry Forecast*, June 1991, p. 38.

about 400 pictures a year. The industry is collecting more money because of higher ticket prices, but the number of people who go to the movies is declining.

The major increase in income to the movie industry in the last decade came from sales of movies for videocassettes. The year 1986 marked the first time that the number of videotape rentals was higher than the number of movie tickets. Industry income is expected to remain unchanged.

Recordings. Prerecorded cassettes account for more than half the recordings sold. Another 30 percent of sales comes from compact discs. Most recordings are bought by people who are under 30. The introduction of digital tapes by the Japanese could change the recordings market. The industry is expected to grow at a rate of about 5 percent, boosted by sales of compact discs.

Book Publishing. Publishers issue about 40,000 titles a year in the United States, although some of these are reprints and new editions of old titles. About 20,000 retail bookstores are in business in the United States, and these bookstores account for 30 percent of all the money earned from book sales. The rest of the books are sold through book clubs, in college stores, to libraries, and to school districts for use in elementary and high schools. Book publishing income is expected to increase at an annual rate of about 4 percent.

Overall, media industries in the United States are prospering. The division of profits is shifting, however, as different media industries expand and contract in the marketplace to respond to the audience. For example, if the population's interest shifts away from the print media to video entertainment, fewer people will buy newspapers, magazines, and books, which means that these industries could suffer. (For recent trends in consumers' media spending, see Figure 1.4.) Understanding the implications of these changes is central to understanding the business of the media.

2. The Media and Communications Technology

The second theme that you will encounter throughout this book is *the effect of technological change on the mass media.* The development of communications technology directly affects the speed with which a society evolves. An entire country with one telephone or one radio may be impossible for people in the United States to imagine, but there are still many countries today where ten families share a single telephone and people consider a television set to be a luxury.

In the United States and other countries such as Japan that have encouraged technological advancements, communications changes are moving faster than ever before. For the media industries, this means increasing costs to replace old equipment. For consumers, this means a confusing array of products that seem to be replaced as soon as they are marketed—compact discs overcoming cassettes, for example.

By today's standards, the earliest communications obstacles seem unbelievably simple: for instance, how to transmit a single message to several people at the same time, and how to share information inexpensively. Yet it has taken nearly 5,500 years to achieve the capability for instant communication that we enjoy today.

Three Communications Revolutions. The channels of communication have changed dramatically over the centuries, but the idea that a society will pay to stay informed and entertained is not new. In imperial Rome, people who wanted to know the news paid professional speakers a coin *(gazet)* for the privilege of listening to the speaker announce the day's events. Many early newspapers were called gazettes to reflect this heritage.

The first attempt at written communication began modestly with pictographs. A pictograph is a symbol of an object that is used to convey an idea. If you have ever drawn a heart with an arrow through it, you understand what a pictograph is. The first known pictographs were carved in stone by the Sumerians of Mesopotamia in about 3500 B.C.

The stone in which these early pictographic messages were carved served as a medium—a device to transmit messages. Eventually, messages were imprinted in clay and stored in a primitive version of today's library. These messages weren't very portable, however. Clay tablets didn't slip easily into someone's pocket.

In about 2500 B.C., the Egyptians invented papyrus, a type of paper made from a grasslike plant called sedge. The Greeks perfected parchment, made from goat and sheep skins, in about 200 B.C. By about A.D.100, before the use of parchment spread throughout Europe, the Chinese had invented paper, which was much cheaper to produce than parchment, but Europeans didn't start to use paper until more than a thousand years later, about A.D. 1300. The discovery of parchment and then paper meant that storing information became cheaper and easier.

Meanwhile, pictographs as a method of communication developed into phonetic writing, using symbols for sounds. Instead of drawing a representation of a dog to convey the idea of a dog, scholars could represent the sounds d-o-g with phonetic writing. The invention of writing has been called the *first information communications revolution.* "After being stored in written form, information could now reach a new kind of audience, remote from the source and uncontrolled by it," writes media scholar Anthony Smith. "Writing transformed knowledge into information."

The Three Communications Revolutions

The invention of writing, displayed here on clay tablets, has been called the first communications revolution. Johannes Gutenberg is responsible for the second communications revolution, the invention of movable type. Satellite dishes, which use computer technology to transmit information, represent the third communications revolution.

The Greek philosopher Socrates anticipated the changes that widespread literacy would bring. He argued that knowledge should remain among the privileged classes. Writing threatened the exclusive use of information, he said: "Once a thing is put in writing, the composition, whatever it may be, drifts all over the place, getting into the hands not only of those who understand it, but equally of those who have no business with it."

As Socrates predicted, when more people learned to write, wider communication became possible because people in many different societies could share information among themselves and with people in other parts of the world. But scholars still had to painstakingly copy the information they wanted to keep, or pay a scribe to copy it for them. In the 14th century, for example, the library of the Italian poet Petrarch contained more than 100 manuscripts that he had copied individually himself.

In Petrarch's day, literate people were either monks or members of the privileged classes. Wealthy people could afford tutoring, and they could also afford to buy the handwritten manuscripts copied by the monks. Knowledge—and the power it brings—belonged to very few people.

As societies grew more literate, the demand for manuscripts flourished, but a scribe could produce only one copy at a time. What has been called the *second information communications revolution* began in Germany in 1455, when Johannes Gutenberg printed a Bible on a press that used movable type.

More than 200 years before Gutenberg, the Chinese had invented a printing press that used wood type, and the Chinese also are credited with perfecting a copper press in 1445. But Gutenberg's innovation was to line up individual metal letters that he could ink and then press with paper to produce copies. Unlike wood or copper, the metal could be reused to produce new pages of text, which made the process much cheaper. The Gutenberg Bible, a duplicate of the Latin original, is considered the first book printed by movable type (47 copies survive).

As other countries adopted Gutenberg's press, the price for Bibles plummeted. In 1470, the cost of a French mechanically printed Bible was one-fifth the cost of a hand-printed Bible. This second revolution—printing—meant that knowledge, which had belonged to the privileged few, would one day be accessible to everyone. This key development was one of the essential conditions for the rise of modern governments, as well as an important element of scientific and technological progress.

Before the Gutenberg press, a scholar who wanted special information had to travel to the place where it was kept. But once information could be duplicated easily, it could travel to people beyond the society that created it. The use of paper instead of the scribes' bulky parchment also meant that books could be stacked end to end. For the first time, knowledge was portable and storable. Libraries now could store vast amounts of information in a small space. And because these smaller lightweight books could be easily carried, classical works could be read simultaneously in many cities by all different kinds of people. Another benefit of the development of printing was that societies could more easily keep information to share with future generations.

This effort to communicate—first through spoken messages, then through pictographs, then through the written word, and finally through printed words—demonstrates people's innate desire to share information with one another. *Storability, portability,* and *accessibility* of information are essential to today's concept of mass communication. By definition, mass communication is information that is available to a large audience quickly.

Today's age of communication has been called the *third information communications revolution* because computers have become the storehouses and transmitters of vast amounts of information that previously relied on the written word. Computer technology, which processes and transmits information much more efficiently than mechanical devices, is driving the majority of changes affecting today's media. This means that changes in today's media industries happen much faster than in the past. Satellite broadcasts, digital recordings, and desktop publishing are just three examples of the third information communications revolution.

Although each medium has its own history and economic structure, today all the media industries compete for consumers' attention. Before the century ends, satellite and microchip technology will transform the media business more than we can foresee—quicker transmission of more information to more people than ever before.

3. The Media and Government

No institution as sizable and influential as the mass media can escape involvement with government and politics. The media are not only channels for the transmission of political information and debate, but also significant players with a direct stake in government's regulatory and economic policies, as well as government's attitude toward free speech and dissent.

Accordingly, the third theme of this book is that *the way a country's political system is organized affects the way the media within that country operate.* Media systems can be divided into those that allow dissent and those that do not. To categorize the political organization of media systems, scholars often begin with the 1956 book *Four Theories of the Press,* by Fred S. Siebert, Theodore Peterson, and Wilbur Schramm. These four theories, which were originally used to describe the political systems under which media operated in different countries, were: (1) the Soviet theory, (2) the authoritarian theory, (3) the libertarian theory, and (4) the social responsibility theory.

The Soviet Theory.   Historically in the Soviet Union, the government owned and operated the mass media. All media employees were government employees, expected to serve the government's interests.

Top media executives also served as leaders in the Communist party. Even when the press controls loosened in the 1980s under *glasnost,* the mass media were *part* of the government's policy. Under the Soviet theory, government control came *before* the media published or broadcast; the people who controlled the media reviewed copy and looked at programs before they appeared.

This description of the Soviet press system was conceived before the events of the 1990s challenged the basic assumptions of Soviet government. Many Eastern bloc countries, such as Romania and Czechoslovakia, which once operated under Soviet influence, based their media systems on the Soviet model. Today, the media systems in these countries are in transition (see Chapter 15).

The Authoritarian Theory.   Media that operate under the authoritarian theory can be either publicly or privately owned. This concept of the press developed in Europe after Gutenberg. Until the 1850s, presses in Europe were privately owned, and the aristocracy (who governed the countries) wanted some sort of control over what was printed about them. The aristocracy had the financial and political power necessary to make the rules about what would be printed.

Their first idea was to license everyone who owned a press so the license could be revoked if someone published something unfavorable about the government. The first colonial newspapers in America, for example, were licensed by the British crown. Licensing wasn't very successful in the United States, however, because many people who owned presses didn't apply for licenses.

The next authoritarian attempt to control the press was to review material after it was published. A printer who was discovered publishing material that strongly challenged the government could be heavily fined or even put to death.

Today, many governments still maintain this type of rigid control over the media. Most monarchies, for example, operate in an authoritarian tradition, which tolerates very little dissent. Media systems that serve at the government's pleasure and with the government's approval are common.

The Libertarian Theory. The concept of a libertarian press evolved from the idea that people who are given all the information on an issue will be able to discern what is true and what is false and will make good choices. This is an idea embraced by the writers of the U.S. Constitution and by other democratic governments.

This theory assumes, of course, that the media's main goal is to convey the truth and that the media will not cave in to outside pressures, such as from advertisers or corporate owners. This theory also assumes that people with opposing viewpoints will be heard—that the media will present all points of view, in what is commonly called the free marketplace of ideas.

The First Amendment to the U.S. Constitution concisely advocates the idea of freedom of the press. Theoretically, America today operates under the libertarian theory, although this ideal has been challenged often by changes in the media industries since the Constitution was adopted.

The Social Responsibility Theory. This theory accepts the concept of a libertarian press but prescribes what the media should do. Someone who believes in the social responsibility theory believes that members of the press will do their jobs well only if periodically reminded about their duties.

This theory grew out of the 1947 Hutchins Commission Report on the Free and Responsible Press. The commission listed five goals for the press, including the need for truthful and complete reporting of all sides of an issue. The commission concluded that the American press' privileged position in the Constitution means that the press must always work to be responsible to society.

If the media fail to meet their responsibilities to society, the social responsibility theory holds that the government should encourage the media to comply. In this way the libertarian and the social responsibility theories differ. The libertarian theory assumes the media will work well without government interference; the social responsibility theory advocates government oversight for media that don't act in society's best interest.

Since 1956 when the four theories first were used to describe media systems, critics have contended that these theories are too limiting and that the categories cannot neatly describe all the world's media. In fact, many countries today combine elements of one or more types of media systems.

Developmental Theory. A fifth description for media systems that can be added to describe today's media has been called the *developmental* or Third World theory. Under this system, named for the developing nations where it is most often found, the media *can* be privately owned, but are usually owned by the government. The media are used to promote the country's social and economic goals, and to direct a sense of national purpose. For example, a developmental media system might be used to promote birth control or to encourage children to attend school. The media become an outlet for certain types of government propaganda, then, but in the name of economic and social progress for the country.

Although the theory that best describes the American media is the libertarian theory, throughout their history the American media have struggled with both authoritarian and social responsibility debates: Should the press be free to print secret government documents, for example? What responsibility do the networks have to provide worthwhile programming to their audiences? The media, the government, and the public continually modify and adjust their interpretations of just how the American media should operate.

4. Media, Society, and Culture

The media industries, as already discussed, provide information and entertainment. But media also can be used to try to persuade the public, and media can affect the culture. These last two functions of media—*persuasion* and *transmission of the culture*—form the basis of the scholarly studies that address the effects media have on society and the culture in which they operate.

This question of the *impact* of the media leads to the fourth theme of this book: *The mass media are cultural institutions that both reflect and affect the society in which they operate.* Although the media can actively influence society, they also mirror it, and scholars constantly strive to delineate the differences.

When the advertising industry suddenly marched to patriotic themes by using flags and other patriotic logos in ads following the United States' claim of victory in the 1991 Gulf War, was the industry pandering, or were advertisers proudly reflecting genuine American sentiment, or both? Did the spread of patriotic themes silence those who felt that the United States overreacted in the Persian Gulf ? If you were a scholar, how would you prove your arguments?

This is an example of the difficulty scholars face when analyzing the media's social and cultural effects. Early media studies analyzed the message in the belief that, once a message was sent, it would be received by everyone the same way. Then studies proved that different people perceived messages differently (described as **selective perception**). This is because everyone brings many variables to each message: family background, interests, and education, for example.

Complicating the study of the media's cultural and social effects is the recent proliferation of media outlets. These multiplying sources for information and entertainment mean that today very few people share identical mass media environments. This makes it much more difficult for scholars to determine the specific or cumulative effects of mass media on the general population.

Still, the attempts by scholars to describe media's social and cultural role in society are important because, once identified, the effects can be observed. The questions should be posed so we do not become complacent about media in our lives, so we do not become immune to the possibility that our culture may be cumulatively affected by the media in ways we cannot yet define.

IN FOCUS

Introduction to the Mass Media

- According to industry estimates, the average adult spends more than half of his or her waking life with the media.
- The mass media industries in the United States earned $134 billion in 1990 and employed nearly 1.5 million people.
- Communication is the act of sending ideas and attitudes from one person to another. Intrapersonal communication means communication within one person. Interpersonal communication means communication between two people. Mass communication is communication from one person or group of persons through a transmitting device (a medium) to large audiences or markets.
- Many motives shape the American media, including the desire to fulfill the public's need for information, to influence the country's governance, to disseminate the country's culture, to offer entertainment, and to provide an outlet for creative expression. But, above all, the major goal of the American media is to make money.
- Four key themes can be used to study American Media:
  1. American media operate as profit-centered businesses;
  2. The media are greatly affected by technological changes;
  3. The way a country's political system is organized affects the way the media within that country operate;
  4. The mass media are cultural institutions that both reflect and affect the society in which they operate.
- Although many media businesses are still family-owned, the main trend in the United States today is for media companies to cluster together in groups. This trend is called concentration of ownership and can take five forms: chains, networks, cross-media ownership, conglomerates, and vertical integration.
- Media acquisitions in the United States have skyrocketed because most conglomerates today are publicly traded companies and because, beginning in 1980, the federal government deregulated the broadcast industry.
- U. S. media industries continue to prosper, but the share of profits is shifting among the industries; different media expand and contract in the marketplace to respond to the audience.
- The communications revolution occurred in three stages. The invention of symbols was considered the first communications revolution; the invention of movable type marked the second communications revolution; and the invention of computers ushered in the third communications revolution.
- Storability, portability, and accessibility of information are essential to today's concept of mass communication. By definition, mass communication is information that is available to a large audience quickly.
- The way a country's political system is organized affects the way the media within that country operate. The traditional four theories of the press divided media systems into the Soviet theory, the authoritarian theory, the libertarian theory, and the social responsibility theory. Recent scholarship has added a fifth theory: the developmental, or Third World, theory.

Gender
Stereotypes and Roles
Third Edition

Susan A. Basow
Lafayette College

Brooks/Cole Publishing Company
Pacific Grove, California

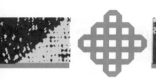

Generally, when we talk about masculinity and femininity, we are talking about certain personality and social characteristics. Females are seen as emotional, submissive, talkative, aware of others' feelings, and so forth; males are seen as possessing opposite traits. Figure 3.1 exemplifies one part of the stereotype.

In examining the factual bases for stereotypes in the areas of personality and social behavior, a number of difficulties arise. Although research problems can and do plague all areas of gender research, there are particular problems we need to be aware of in reviewing research on personality and social behavior. First, we need to remember that situational factors interact with individual factors in determining behavior. Thus, it is inaccurate to speak of social traits, such as assertiveness existing solely within the individual. A person in isolation is not assertive.

A second problem arises when social behavior must be operationally defined—that is, described in terms of objective measurement. Although cognitive differences, such as verbal ability, can be measured by a variety of paper-and-pencil tests (for example, spelling, reading comprehension), it is much more difficult operationally to define and measure concepts like dependence, which can refer to clinging behaviors, social responsiveness, number of friends, and so forth. If researchers use different definitions of the same concept, the results are difficult to compare.

A variety of person-related problems must also be considered. Many social behaviors and the way they are measured change as a function of age. Thus, it is important to take the age of the participants into account in comparing studies and in drawing conclusions. For example, research done with college students, generally aged 18 to 22, may not accurately generalize to all adults. Similarly, findings from research based on male participants may not accurately be generalized to females, as many researchers have done (for example, Kohlberg, 1969). A related problem occurs when research on White participants is generalized to people of different racial and ethnic backgrounds. Especially in the area of social behavior, different ethnic and racial groups may demonstrate different patterns (for example, K. A. Adams, 1980, 1983).

It is important to recognize the tremendous range of individual differences in the area of personality and social behavior. Such differences overshadow any gender-based ones. Thus, clear-cut differences between males and females are difficult to find and of little use in predicting an individual's performance.

The behaviors discussed in this chapter can be grouped into four major areas: personality and temperament, communication patterns, prosocial behaviors (those that facilitate interpersonal relationships), and power-related behaviors. Although much overlap occurs among these four areas, the prosocial and power distinction parallels those made by personality theorists (for example, Buss & Finn, 1987) as well as the stereotypic view of women as being more interpersonal and of men as being more agentic or active. We will come across a number of common themes: the importance of gender as opposed to sex, the importance of person-situation interactions, and the importance of race of subject.

Personality and Temperament

The term *personality* refers to the distinctive character of an individual, which includes traits, behaviors, emotions, and thoughts, whereas *temperament* refers to emotional mood or disposition only. Both areas have been assumed to show gender differences. Most personality theorists, however, emphasize individual, rather than sex-specific, differences. Psychodynamic theorists, starting with Freud, are exceptions. For our purposes, a brief look at personality development as related to sex typing will prove instructive.

PERSONALITY DEVELOPMENT

When one talks about personality development, the distinction between stereotypic gender differences and true gender differences often is difficult to determine. As noted in Chapter 1, people generally are in a great deal of agreement as to what constitutes the gender stereotypes, and these stereotypes are learned by ages 3 to 5. However, children do not necessarily behave accordingly. In particular, girls show much less behavioral sex typing than boys (Maccoby & Jacklin, 1974; Stericker & Kurdek, 1982; Urberg, 1982). Between ages 3 and 11, it is very unusual for boys to prefer activities or toys ascribed to girls, but it is quite common for girls to choose "boys'" toys and activities. In fact, between ages 6 and 9, most girls prefer "male" activities, perhaps because such activities are more interesting or more fun.

In contrast to behavioral sex typing, sex-typed personality traits are slower to develop in boys than in girls, perhaps because the traits associated with masculinity are relatively more adult and perhaps unnatural than the traits associated with femininity (S. W. Davis, Williams, & Best, 1982; Stericker & Kurdek, 1982). For example, the independent, assertive, and unemotional parts of the male stereotype are difficult for most children and, perhaps, for most adults to acquire. With puberty come increased societal pressures to conform to gender expectations. From grades 6 to 12, increasing consistency between self-description and sex-role expectations is found (Donelson, 1977; Feather, 1984). These gender differences conform to the two sets of stereotypes discussed in Chapter 1, variously labeled as expressive and instrumental (Parsons & Bales, 1955) or communal and agentic (Bakan, 1966). After grade 7, females tend to rate themselves significantly higher than males on expressive-nurturant traits; males tend to rate themselves significantly higher than females on instrumental-active traits, differences that have been quite stable despite societal changes over the last 30 years (R. O. Baldwin, 1984; Galambos, Almeida, & Petersen, 1990). These results hold true for Blacks as well as Whites, at least among college students (R. O. Baldwin, 1987). Nonetheless, recent research does suggest that gender differences with respect to instrumental-active traits are decreasing (Gill, Stockard, Johnson, & Williams, 1987; Snell, 1989). Remaining are gender differences in the expressive-relational dimension.

With gender stereotypes being as pervasive as they are, it is not surprising that most people see themselves as behaving in gender-appropriate ways. Whether they actually behave this way is a different matter. This question will be the focus of the rest of the chapter. Even when behavioral differences are found, they are as or more likely to be due to situational factors, differential learning opportunities, or societal rewards as to differences in personality.

The question of the causal sequence between personality and behavior is an important one. Given the pervasive pattern of women rating themselves higher than men on expressive-communal qualities and men rating themselves higher than women on instrumental-agentic qualities, it is easy to view these traits as being innate, or at least basic to women and men. It therefore seems to follow that gender differences in personality *cause* gender differences in behavior. However, as discussed in Chapter 1 (see Figure 1.2), it is just as likely that gender differences in behavior *cause* gender differences in personality. That is, it is because of the particular roles each sex plays and thereby the distinctive situations each sex encounters that different traits develop (Deaux & Major, 1987; Eagly, 1987b; Epstein, 1988). For example, individuals who spend a large amount of time caring for others, especially young children, will be encouraged to develop nurturant and expressive traits. Individuals who spend a large amount of time in a competitive hierarchical employment situation will be encouraged to develop agentic and assertive traits. In cross-cultural research, Whiting and Edwards (1988) found just that: an individual who spends enough time with infants will become a nurturer. In most but not all cultures, it is females who spend much time with infants.

Not only do females in North America take care of young children more than do males, but during adolescence, girls and boys spend much of their spare time doing different things as well (Timmer, Eccles, & O'Brien, 1985). Adolescent girls spend much more time than their male peers doing household work and grooming activities, while adolescent boys spend much more time than their female peers engaged in sports. These different activities, conforming as they do to gender stereotypes, may encourage different traits and behaviors to develop. For example, participation in sports may facilitate competitive traits more than does housework.

This view of roles and experiences as affecting personality also fits in with certain developmental findings. Although most research concentrates on children and college students, personality development continues throughout the life span. When personality development is defined in terms of ego development (increasingly complex perceptions of the self and others; Loevinger, 1976), gender differences increase from childhood to early adolescence (around age 13), remain moderately large during adolescence, then decline among college students to essentially no difference among the post-college-aged (Cohn, 1991). The direction of the difference favors females, who consistently score about one stage higher than males in maturity as they go from impulsiveness, to self-protection, to social conformity, to self-awareness, to conscientiousness, and finally to individuality and autonomy (few reach this last stage). The different social experiences of children and adolescents noted earlier seem the most likely explanation for these developmental patterns.

A number of studies report that people tend to become more androgynous (that is, combine both expressive and agentic competencies) as they mature from late adolescence to middle adulthood (Gutmann, 1987; Jung, 1956; Levinson, 1978; V. Mitchell & Helson, 1990). Men appear to become more acceptant of communal-expressive characteristics with age, while women appear to become more agentic and confident. The process, however, may not be linear. Women college graduates appear to become more feminine-sex-typed during their 20s as they prepare for or engage in parenting (Helson & Moane, 1987). However, these same women become more androgynous between their late 20s and mid 40s as their child-rearing days recede. Thus, it is important to speak cautiously of generalized gender differences in personality across the life span.

Despite strong evidence that gender differences in personality are a function of gender differences in social expectations, experiences, and roles, and are most apparent starting at adolescence, many believe gender differences in personality are either biological or arise from early childhood experiences. The biological evidence is tentative and stems from recent research with twins and adolescents. One study found genetics accounted for 20% to 48% of the observed individual differences in instrumental-active and nurturant-expressive traits in a sample of twins aged 8 to 14 (J. E. Mitchell, Baker, & Jacklin, 1989). The remaining 52% to 80% of the variance was due to environmental influences specific to each individual. Replication of these findings, especially with twins at different ages and who were reared apart, is needed. Another study attempted to link sex-typed traits with hormonal changes at puberty (Udry & Talbert, 1988). Although some sex-linked personality traits were found to be correlated with testosterone level (traits such as dominance, outgoingness, sensitivity, and understanding), gender differences in testosterone level did not explain gender differences in personality since girls are much more sensitive than boys to this hormone. Furthermore, other research that has attempted to link pubertal timing with increased sex typing of personality traits has found little support (Galambos et al., 1990). Thus, biological explanations of gender difference in personality are still speculative at this time.

Nonetheless, a number of personality theorists, mainly psychodynamic ones, do posit basic gender differences in personality. Freud suggested that anatomical differences combined with psychosexual dynamics lead girls and boys to develop different personality traits by age 5 or 6 (this theory will be discussed in more depth in Chapters 4 and 6). Because Freud thought that the penis was the intrinsically superior sex organ, he stated that boys' recognition that they had one, and that girls did not, led boys to feel superior and to develop active-autonomous traits at the resolution of the phallic stage of psychosexual development. At the same time, according to Freud, both boys and girls develop their gender identity after identifying with the same-sex parent. In this view, girls must identify with someone who has an inferior sex organ, and therefore girls develop feelings of inferiority and traits of vanity, passivity, and dependence; feelings and traits that are "normal" and "natural." This aspect of Freud's theory has very little empirical support, as we will see in other chapters. Nonetheless, it figures prominently in cultural theories of gender differences.

More recently, feminist psychodynamic theories (for example, Chodorow, 1978, 1990; J. B. Miller, 1976, 1984) have posited basic gender differences in personality due to the fact that it is mainly women who raise children. According to these theories, girls develop their sense of self, which starts to emerge during the first year of life, in the context of a relationship with a similar other. In contrast, boys experience a disjunction between their first "object" of attachment and their own developing sense of self. Consequently, boys develop an identity characterized by independence and autonomous strivings and a rejection of the feminine, whereas girls develop an identity characterized by interpersonal involvement and empathy. Direct empirical tests of these theories are sorely lacking, but their implications with respect to gender differences in behaviors and attitudes are far-reaching. We will evaluate these theories further as we examine specific personal and social behaviors.

TEMPERAMENT

With regard to temperament, females have often been thought to be more passive than males. However, the term *passivity* can mean a variety of different things: submissiveness, lack of sexual interest, dependence, inactivity, and so on. From the research on the possible components of passivity, it is clear that little support exists for the assumption that females are uniformly more passive than males.

Among researchers, *temperament* generally refers to basic emotional dispositions. Studies of infants show few consistent gender differences in the area of emotionality, but male infants do appear to be more irritable, emotionally labile, less attentive, and less socially responsive than female infants (Haviland & Malatesta, 1982; Maccoby & Jacklin, 1974; D. Phillips et al., 1978). The situations that occasion emotional outbursts are different for boys and for girls from age 3 to 5. Boys react most to frustration situations, conflicts with adults, and fear-inducing situations; girls respond most to conflicts with other children. Girls also decrease their total emotional responsiveness at a faster rate than boys.

Among adolescents, boys and girls experience the same intensity of emotions but differ with respect to the types of emotions they feel most strongly and most frequently and the context in which these emotions occur. In one study (Stapley & Haviland, 1989), 5th graders through 11th graders rated 3 (out of 12) emotions as most salient—joy, interest, and anger. Girls reported somewhat greater salience than boys of negative emotions, especially sadness, shyness, shame, guilt, and self-hostility. On the other hand, contempt was more salient for boys than girls. Boys and girls also differed with respect to emotional contexts. Girls found affiliation events to be associated with the strongest emotions; boys found activities and achievement events to be associated with the strongest emotions. Thus, it's not that girls experience more intense emotions than boys, but that the types of and contexts giving rise to emotions differ by gender.

Perhaps because females report more sadness than males, females also report crying significantly more frequently and intensely than males, and in a wider variety of situations (Lombardo, Cretser, Lombardo, & Mathis, 1983). However, both males and females agree on the kinds of situations in which crying is most likely to occur. Why females may in fact be sadder than males will be discussed in Chapter 8, when the effects of gender roles on mental health, and in particular depression, are examined.

A small tendency has been found for girls to be more timid than boys in early childhood (Jacklin, Maccoby, & Doering, 1983). Girls also consistently report more fears than boys and are rated as more fearful by others (W. K. Silverman & Nelles, 1987). However, observational studies do not show females, in childhood and adolescence, actually to evidence more timid behaviors than males of that age (L. R. Brody, 1984; Maccoby & Jacklin, 1974). This apparent gender difference in fearfulness may be a function of sex typing, since reported fears correlate significantly with femininity scores (L. R. Brody, Hay, & Vandewater, 1990; Krasnoff, 1981). The difference in fearfulness also may be a function of gender expectations. Girls, especially those high in "feminine" traits, may be more likely to admit to fear or anxieties because such admissions are more socially acceptable from, and more expected of, them.

In this regard, Birnbaum and colleagues (Birnbaum & Croll, 1984; Birnbaum, Nosanchuk, & Croll, 1980) found that preschoolers had marked stereotypes about sex differences in emotionality. Females were more associated with fear, sadness, and happiness, and males were more associated with anger. Similar stereotypes were held by parents and were reflected in television programming. Parents, in practice, accepted anger in boys more than in girls and accepted fear in girls more than in boys. Thus, girls actually may show more fear than boys because fear is more socially acceptable for girls than boys. These stereotypes may also lead more females than males to report fearfulness. The equation of fear with femininity also may explain why males often engage in risk-taking activities to prove that they are not fearful; that is, not feminine.

Thus, in terms of emotionality, male infants appear somewhat more emotionally expressive than female infants, but these differences disappear and then reverse themselves during grade school and adolescence, especially for the specific emotions of fear and sadness. With respect to anger and hostility, however, girls increasingly inhibit displaying and even recognizing such emotions. A curious aspect of research in this area is defining emotionality solely as fear or as the number of emotional upsets. Emotions, of course, cover a wide range of feelings, including hostility. Yet, although more males than females display and report hostile feelings, males are rarely described as "emotional," as illustrated in Figure 3.1. We need to recognize that the term *emotion* is itself socially constructed (Shields,1987).

The developmental pattern just noted suggests that socialization practices may actively work to encourage boys to minimize or mask their emotional expressiveness. For example, Buck (1977) found that boys between ages 4 and 6 increasingly inhibited and masked their overt reactions to emotion-producing situations (in this case, slides depicting emotion-laden scenes). Girls, however, continued to respond relatively freely to such situations. Such differences, becoming more extreme during adolescence, clearly conform to gender stereotypes of females as being emotional. This developmental pattern suggests that gender differences in emotional expressiveness may be more a consequence of gender socialization and social roles than a basis for them. Research on socialization practices supports this conclusion (Balswick, 1988; L. R. Brody, 1985; Fivush, 1989).

In sum, it is not accurate to say that females are more emotional than males. Much depends on the definition of emotionality used, the age group studied, the social context, and the specific emotions examined. Females do appear to be more emotionally expressive than males with respect to most emotions except anger. This gender difference in emotional expressivity is related to gender differences in communication patterns, to which we now turn.

Communication Patterns

The stereotype of female emotionality may be related to the greater frequency with which females display or communicate their emotions. The area of communication is an extremely important one in the study of gender, since most of our information and knowledge of others comes through their verbal or nonverbal cues. In ground-breaking work, Nancy Henley (1977; Mayo & Henley, 1981) found gender differences in communication patterns to be pervasive in both verbal and nonverbal behaviors.

VERBAL COMMUNICATION

Overall, males tend to dominate verbally and females tend to listen. Contradicting the "talkative female" stereotype, Henley and others (for example, Aries,1987; Lakoff,1975) have found that males talk more and for longer periods of time than females. Males interrupt other speakers more, control the topic of conversations more, make more jokes, speak less in standard English (that is, they use slang more), and more often use a familiar form of address (first name, "honey") when talking to a female than would a female talking to a male. Females talk at a much higher pitch, allow themselves to be interrupted more, listen more, and disclose more personal information to others. Women more than men use tag questions ("It's hot, isn't it?"), qualifiers ("maybe," "I guess"), and compound requests ("Won't you close the window?" rather than "Close the window"). These three speech style differences are assumed to indicate a lack of assertiveness and more politeness on the part of females. Indeed, women are expected to be polite in their speech, regardless of the gender of the person addressed or the content of the speech (Kemper, 1984). In contrast, males are expected to modify their speech as a function of the gender-appropriateness of the content and the gender of the addressee. For example, it is rarely all right for women to use profanity, but men can use it as long as they don't use it with women. The use of profanity by males appears to demonstrate a degree of social power that women do not have (Selnow, 1985).

These gendered linguistic patterns appear early in life and increase in frequency with age. Even among preschoolers, males tend to talk more, initiate more topics, and use more attention-getting speech devices than their female peers (Austin, Salehi, & Leffler, 1987; Cook, Fritz, McCornack, & Visperas, 1985). In contrast, young girls' speech uses more conversation facilitators and reinforcers than boys' speech. Research on parental directives to young children suggests that children learn these different linguistic styles from their parents (Bellinger & Gleason,1982). For example, fathers appear to issue more direct commands than mothers ("Put the screw in"), and mothers appear to issue more indirect requests than fathers ("Can you put the screw in?"). Cross-cultural research confirms that gender differences in language use, although fairly universal, are socially constructed (Philips, Steele, & Tanz, 1987).

Differences in content of conversation are not clear because males and females often engage in different activities and occupations. Content differences also are unclear because content of conversation appears to depend not only on the gender of the speaker but also on the gender of the listener (Haas, 1981; J. A. Hall & Braunwald, 1981). Among White middle-class children, boys talk more about sports to both boys and girls, and girls talk to girls more about school, identity, and wishing and needing. When girls talk to boys, they are more verbally compliant and they laugh more. When boys talk to girls, they use more direct requests. College women talk more frequently about a third person than do college men, but there is no gender difference in the frequency of derogatory remarks about that person (Levin & Arluke,1985). In general, males more often are talked about by both sexes, perhaps a reflection of their greater importance or interest.

With respect to self-disclosure of intimate information, such as personality and bodily matters, women are more self-disclosing than men (Balswick, 1988; Derlega, Durham, Gockel, & Sholis, 1981; C. T. Hill & Stull, 1987). However, when personal topics are considered neutral, such as tactfulness, or masculine, such as aggressiveness, no gender difference regularly appears. With respect to feelings, men are less expressive of positive emotions than negative ones (Saurer & Eisler, 1990).

Why are men less likely than women to disclose positive feelings and personal information about themselves? The answer seems to be that such behaviors are seen as feminine, revealing emotionality and vulnerability (E. T. Lewis & McCarthy, 1988). As such, they may be considered socially unacceptable for males. Indeed, it is only the men who are experiencing gender role stress or who are low in expressive-nurturant traits (masculine and undifferentiated males) who limit their disclosure of positive emotions and personal information (Lavine & Lombardo, 1984; Narus & Fischer, 1982; Saurer & Eisler,1990). Androgynous people of both sexes appear to be flexible with regard to self-disclosure, responding more to their partner's level of disclosure and to the nature of the topic than their sex-typed peers (Sollie & Fischer, 1985).

Certain aspects of the masculine gender role, such as restrictive emotionality and inhibited affection, clearly work against intimate self-disclosure (Snell, Miller, Belk, Garcia-Falconi, & Hernandez-Sanchez, 1989). The association of intimate self-disclosure with femininity suggests that the social costs and rewards of such behavior will differ for males and females. This was demonstrated in a study by Derlega and Chaikin (1976), who found that self-disclosing college men were perceived by college students of both sexes as significantly more psychologically maladjusted than non-self-disclosing men. For women, however, the reverse was true; that is, the non-self-disclosing women were seen as significantly more maladjusted.

Overall, the type of verbal communication typical of men (verbal dominance, direct statements, limited intimate self-disclosure) reflects men's greater social dominance and their concern with power and competition. Men use talk to negotiate and maintain their higher status. Reciprocally, the type of verbal communication typical of women (listening, qualifying, politeness, personal self-disclosure) reflects women's relative subordination and greater interpersonal involvement. Women use talk to signal support and to maintain relationships. The outcome of these different styles and goals may be problems in male-female communication (Tannen, 1990). Social perception research confirms the effects of these different communication styles: the "feminine" linguistic style is perceived by others of both sexes as higher in social warmth but lower in competence and assertiveness than the "nonfeminine" linguistic style (Mulac, Incontro, & James, 1985; Quina, Wingard, & Bates, 1987). Given the social functions different linguistic styles support, it is not surprising that people who deviate from these gender expectations would be socially denigrated. For example, men who use the "female" linguistic style are perceived by others of both sexes as homosexual; women who use the "male" style are perceived as uppity (Rasmussen & Moely, 1986).

NONVERBAL COMMUNICATION

In studies of nonverbal behavior, the observed gender differences are of even greater importance than in the verbal behaviors just noted, since the impact of nonverbal communication is so much stronger and so much more subtle than verbal communication (Henley & Thorne, 1977). Generally, females are more restricted in their demeanor and personal space, have more frequent eye contact during conversations (but avoid eye contact otherwise), smile more when it is unrelated to happiness, touch less in impersonal settings but are touched more, and are more sensitive to nonverbal cues than males (J. A. Hall, 1984, 1987; Henley, 1977; Mayo & Henley, 1981). The size of the gender differences in this area is medium to large. Few of these differences appear among children, however, and many of these general findings must be qualified by situational, cultural, and sex-typing factors.

For example, the finding related to females' skill at decoding nonverbal cues is complex. Although above-average ability in decoding is found in 61% of females and 39% of males $(d = .43)$, research suggests that this superiority is present mainly when the nonverbal message appears to be intentional and overt, such as in facial expressions, rather than more covert or unintended, such as in body position (Blanck, Rosenthal, Snodgrass, DePaulo, & Zuckerman, 1981; Rosenthal & DePaulo, 1979). The interpretation of this pattern has been in terms of "politeness"; that is, females learn to refrain from effectively decoding the less controllable cues of the sender. The finding that this pattern increases with age from the year 9 to 21 suggests that this phenomenon results from social learning; that is, girls may be trained through modeling and rewards to develop this decoding pattern.

As was found with verbal behaviors, males are less expressive nonverbally than are females, a gender difference that appears regularly among adults but inconsistently among children (Buck, 1977; J. A. Hall, 1984; Haviland & Malatesta, 1982; Yarczower & Daruns, 1982). Facial expressiveness is one of the largest gender differences found $(d = 1.01)$, with above-average expressiveness characteristic of 75% of females and only 25% of males. The age pattern suggests that learning this skill is part of learning one's gender role, a hypothesis supported by finding a stronger relationship between encoding skill and sex typing than between encoding skill and sex (M. Zuckerman, DeFrank, Spiegel, & Larrance, 1982). Accuracy of encoding intentional nonverbal cues is positively correlated with expressive ("feminine") traits, and negatively correlated with instrumental ("masculine") traits.

The importance of sex typing with respect to nonverbal behavior is clearly illustrated by a study conducted by LaFrance and Carmen (1980; LaFrance, 1982). Androgynous and sex-typed male and female undergraduates were observed in same-sex pairs in either a situation requiring instrumental qualities (debating an abstract issue) or expressive qualities (sharing feelings about starting college). Some nonverbal behaviors were coded as feminine (for example, smiling, gazing) and some were coded as masculine (for example, interrupting, vocalizing while pausing "uh . . . ," "mmm . . ."). Both types of nonverbal behaviors were present in androgynous individuals, whereas sex-typed students were more restricted to sex-consonant behaviors, regardless of the topic. Similar results (that non-sex-typed individuals were less sex-typed behaviorally) have been found with respect to how people move their bodies (Frable, 1987). It is interesting that "feminine" language styles have been found to contribute to a communicator's credibility, perhaps because listeners interpret sharing feelings, smiling, and gazing as linked to personal openness. In contrast, "masculine" language styles appear to contribute to the perception of the communicator as extroverted, perhaps because frequent and constant vocalizations are interpreted as a desire to affect the listener (Berryman-Fink & Wilcox, 1983). Thus it may be an advantage to use different speech modes in a flexible fashion, as androgynous individuals seem to do.

One must keep situational cues in mind when discussing all social behaviors, especially nonverbal ones. For example, the gender of the person to whom one talks may be as important as or more important than the gender of the person communicating (M. Davis & Weitz, 1982; J. A. Hall & Braunwald, 1981). Such factors also are important in research on personal space (Berman & Smith, 1984; Hayduk, 1983), smiling (J. A. Hall & Halberstadt, 1986), and touching (Berman & Smith, 1984; Major, Schmidlin, & Williams, 1990; Stier & Hall, 1984).

Another important variable is culture. Females tend to sit closer than males during conversations, but the actual distance varies as a function of cultural background and the language being spoken (N. M. Sussman & Rosenfeld, 1982). The pattern of gender differences in nonverbal behavior just described may be more characteristic of Whites than Blacks. For example, Black women appear to smile and lean less than Black men, look at one another less often than White female pairs, and move together in synchrony more often than both White female and Black male pairs (Halberstadt & Saitta, 1987; A. Smith, 1983). Hispanic females appear less likely than Anglo females to show nonverbal behaviors indicative of leadership (for example, physical touch and intrusiveness) (Moore & Porter, 1988).

Still, the general pattern of research suggests that females nonverbally display more submission and warmth and males display more dominance and high-status cues (Frieze & Ramsey, 1976).

EXPLANATIONS

Physiological factors and gender-related traits have been suggested to explain gender differences in communication patterns. The main physiological explanation rests on research in hemispheric processing of the brain (see Chapter 2). The right hemisphere appears to be dominant in mediating the perception of emotional material; the left hemisphere, in forming verbal codes for emotion (Saxby & Bryden, 1985). The female advantage in discerning the emotions of others may be due to women's somewhat greater use of both hemispheres. This gender difference, which is quite small, may reflect innate differences in brain structure, or it could come from early conditioning. The age patterns suggest the latter. Because males generally are discouraged from acknowledging their emotions verbally as part of their sex role, fewer males than females may build the necessary hemispheric connections.

Male and female infants may present different patterns of emotional reactivity and different forms of signaling behaviors very early in life (L. R. Brody, 1985; Haviland & Malatesta, 1982; Trotter, 1983). Parents, particularly mothers, may view these behaviors differently as a function of infant gender, with girls' expressions viewed more positively, boys' more negatively. Furthermore, high maternal expressiveness may overstimulate highly reactive infant males. Perhaps as a consequence of these factors, mothers appear to be more restrictive in the range of emotions they express toward and encourage in their sons, as opposed to their daughters. The result would be girls' enhanced understanding of emotional expression.

Although physiological and learning factors may be important in understanding communication behavior, the most persuasive explanations focus on the role and status differences between males and females. The status explanation (first suggested by Hacker, 1951) rests on the assumption that males and females hold different statuses and have differential access to power in our culture. Differences in communication behaviors, then, reflect differences in status and power, and are not specific to gender.

Henley (1977; Mayo & Henley, 1981) has compared gender differences in verbal and nonverbal behavior to differences based on other status dimensions, summarized in Table 3.1. In this scheme, females' politeness, smiling, emotional expressiveness, smaller personal space, less frequent touching and talking, and greater frequency of being interrupted all reflect their subordinate status. Females' greater sensitivity to nonverbal cues may reflect a survival mechanism. Because a female's well-being is likely to depend on her "superior's" moods or desires, it is to her advantage to learn to read them well, especially because these "superiors" try to hide them. Henley's analysis has received some but not unequivocal support (C. E. Brown, Dovidio, & Ellyson, 1990; Halberstadt & Saitta, 1987; Porter & Geis, 1982; Snodgrass,1985; Stier & Hall, 1984). Henley's conclusions apply mainly to adults and are situation-specific. For example, although men tend to display more visual dominance behavior than women, when women are viewed as knowledgeable or expert with respect to a particular task, their visual dominance behavior increases (C. E. Brown et al.,1990; Dovidio, Ellyson, Keating, Heltman, & Brown, 1988).

Gender differences in communication also may reflect gender differences in social roles (Eagly, 1987b). Although gender roles may incorporate a status differential, they involve much more. As described in Chapter 1, the female role emphasizes affiliation aspects whereas the male role emphasizes agentic ones. Thus, gender differences in communication patterns may reflect gender differences in warmth and affiliation (J. A. Hall, 1987; Major et al., 1990).

One problem with the status analysis is that it implies that higher status behaviors are "better" than lower status behaviors. However, an argument can be made that the communication pattern more typical of women has many positive aspects. Because females (or feminine- and androgynous-sex-typed individuals) generally use more self-disclosure, display greater eye contact and smiling behavior, have smaller personal space, and exhibit greater listening and attending skills than males, they generally facilitate close personal interactions. Rosenthal, Hall, DiMatteo, Rogers, and Archer (1979) have determined that people who are more skillful at decoding nonverbal cues are more effective in their interpersonal relationships. Because more women have this skill and use it politely, their proficiency in interpersonal situations is strengthened. Males (or masculine-sex-typed individuals), who have greater domination of conversations, space, and touching, and have minimal self-disclosure, generally impede close personal interactions but facilitate interpersonal control. These differences in spheres of influence (personal interactions versus power interactions) again reflect gender differences in social roles.

In sum, females communicate feelings verbally and nonverbally more than males. In contrast, males communicate dominance and power more than females. These communication patterns seem to serve the different roles assigned women and men—interpersonal and agentic, respectively. Communication styles appear to be learned and are related to both sex-typed characteristics and social status.

Appendix B
Glossary

Academic skills   Special courses offered in colleges and universities to help students improve skills necessary to succeed in college (e.g., writing, reading, math)

Academic year   The period between September and May (or June)

Accreditation   Approval granted after a school has been studied by an official review board and has met its requirements

Adjunct professor   Part-time or temporary faculty member

Advanced placement   Student is placed in a high-level course; allowed to omit courses after passing a qualifying test

Advanced standing   See Advanced placement

Advisor   A professional who offers advice on academic, professional, or personal matters

Alumni   Former students who have graduated from a school

Assistant professor   A college or university professor who ranks below an associate professor

Associate professor   A college or university professor who ranks above an assistant professor and below a full professor

Audit   To attend a college or university course without receiving academic credit

Bursar   The university official in charge of the business office; the university office that collects tuition and fees

Catalog   A list and description of university services, policies, courses, etc.

Chairman or Chairwoman (Chair)   The head of a department

Chancellor   The top official of a college or university system

Community college   A two-year college

Concentration   The principle field of study chosen by a student; major

Credits   The units a student receives after passing a course

Credit hours   The number of units a course is worth

Curriculum   All the courses offered at a school or in a particular department

Deadline   The date when a paper or project must be turned in; due date

Dean   The head of a college or division in a university

Degree   A title given by a college or university when a student has completed his or her studies

    I. Undergraduate degrees:
      A. **Associate**   Two-year degree awarded by community colleges and junior colleges:
        1. **A.A.** (Associate of Arts)
        2. **A.S.** (Associate of Science)
      B. **Bachelor**   Four-year degree awarded by universities:
        1. **B.A.** (Bachelor of Arts)
        2. **B.S.** (Bachelor of Science)
        3. **B.F.A.** (Bachelor of Fine Arts)
    II. Graduate degrees:
      A. **Master**   A degree awarded by universities and professional schools after one or two years of graduate studies:
        1. **M.A.** (Master of Arts)

2. **M.Ed**. (Master of Education)
3. **M.S.** (Master of Science)
4. **M.F.A.** (Master of Fine Arts)
5. **M.B.A.** (Master of Business Administration)
6. **M.L.S.** (Master of Library Sciences)
B. **Doctorate**   A degree awarded by universities and professional schools after three or more years of graduate studies:
1. **Ph.D**. (Doctor of Philosophy)
2. **Ed.D**. (Doctor of Education)
3. **J.D**. (Doctor of Jurisprudence [Law])
4. **M.D**. (Doctor of Medicine)

Department   A particular field of study within a college or university; a unit within a division (e.g., the French Department)

Diagnostic test   A test given to determine a student's level in a particular subject; used for advanced placement

Diploma   A document given by a college or university showing that a student has earned a particular degree

Dissertation   A long, formal research paper written by an advanced degree student; a thesis

Division   A group of departments (e.g., Foreign Languages)

Dormitory   Student housing

Drop/Add period   The time at the beginning of a semester when a student can change courses without penalty

Due date   The date when a paper or project must be turned in; deadline

Elective   A course that is not a requirement

Essay tests   A test in which a student must write an original answer in paragraph form

Faculty   The instructors in a college or university; professors

Fee   Money which is paid for tuition or other school services

Final exam   A major test given at the end of the term

Financial aid   Monetary assistance

Freshman   A first-year undergraduate student

Full professor   The highest-ranked professor at a college or university

General education courses (GE)   Required courses for lower-division students

Grade point average (GPA)   A numerical average used to show a student's academic performance; the average of a 4-point grading system; quality point average

Graduate assistant (GA)   A graduate student who teaches classes or labs or assists professors in research, grading papers, etc.; teaching assistant (TA)

Graduate school   Programs for degrees beyond a bachelor's degree

Graduate student   A student working for a degree beyond a bachelor's degree

Humanities   Fields of study concerning people and culture (e.g., literature, philosophy); not the sciences

Incomplete grade   An *I* on your transcript; if course work was not completed, students will sometimes be given a short period of time to complete the work before the *I* changes to a failing grade

Independent study   A student works independently for academic credit under the guidance of a professor

Junior   A third-year undergraduate student

Junior college   A two-year college

Laboratory (Lab) session   Course time spent in a laboratory doing practical work (e.g., language lab, science lab, psychology lab, etc.)

Leave of absence   A period of time away from school taken with permission

Lecture   A speech about a given topic delivered to a class

Liberal arts   Courses that provide general knowledge about people and culture rather than practical or technical training

Lowerclassmen   Freshmen and sophomores

Lower division   Courses taken by lowerclassmen

Major   The principle field of study chosen by a student; concentration

Matriculation   Official enrollment in a college or university

Mid-term exam   An important exam given in the middle of the term

Minor   A secondary field of study chosen by a student

Natural sciences   Sciences such as biology, chemistry, and physics

Objective test   A test consisting of multiple-choice, true/false, matching, or fill-in-the-blank questions

Office hours   Specific hours set aside by professors to meet with students

Open university   A means by which nonmatriculated students can enroll in courses, space permitting

Oral exams (Orals)   Exams in which a student is tested by verbally answering questions asked by a professor or a panel of professors

Pass/Fail   A grading option that notes whether a student passed or failed a course

Placement test   A qualifying test used for advanced placement; a proficiency test

Plagiarism   Citing the words or ideas of another person without giving credit to the source

Post-graduate   Graduate standing

Practicum   A course that offers students practical experience (e.g., practice teaching)

Prerequisite   A course that is required before you are allowed to take another course

President   The head of a university

Probation   A time period during which a student must improve his or her grades in order to continue studying at a college or university

Professor   The highest ranked instructor at a college or university; full professor

Professor emeritus   A retired professor

Proficiency test   A qualifying test used for advanced placement; a placement test

Provost   Second in command to the president of a university

Quality point average (QPA)   A numerical average used to show a student's academic performance; the average of a 4-point grading system; grade point average

Quarter system   The academic year divided into four sessions

Registrar   A college or university official responsible for students' academic records

Registration   Signing up for academic courses

Research   Academic investigation done in the library, in a lab, or out in the field

Research paper   An academic paper incorporating research

Semester   One of two academic sessions that make up the academic year

Seminar   A small class where students engage in discussion

Senior   A fourth-year undergraduate student

Social sciences   Fields of study related to the study of society and human relationships (e.g., anthropology, sociology, psychology, political science, etc.)

Sophomore   A second-year undergraduate student

Staff   Employees of a college or university who are neither faculty nor administrators

Subjective test   A test in which students are expected to write original answers; essay test

Syllabus   A course description distributed by the professor at the beginning of the term

Take-home exam   A test done outside of class

Teaching assistants (TA)   A graduate student who teaches classes or labs or assists professors in research, grading papers, etc.; graduate assistant (GA)

Tenure   A permanent position on the faculty granted to professors after a set number of years when specific criteria have been met

Term   A period of time in an academic year—a semester, a trimester, or a quarter

Term paper   A research paper

Thesis   A long, formal research paper written by an advanced-degree student; a dissertation

Transcript   An official record of students' grades kept in the registrar's office

Trimester   One of three academic sessions that make up an academic year

Tuition   Money paid to a college or university for instruction

Undergraduate student   A student who has not completed a four-year degree

University   A four-year institution of higher education

Upperclassmen   Juniors and seniors

Upper division   Courses taken by upperclassmen

Withdrawal   Drop a course or leave a college or university

Workshop   A small group of students and instructors who meet to practice a particular skill (e.g., a math workshop)

LIBRARY TERMINOLOGY

Abridged   Reduced in length; condensed (e.g., an abridged dictionary)

Abstract   A brief summary of a book or article

Almanac   An annual publication with lists, charts, and tables of useful information

Archives   Written records of an organization or institution

Article   A report or essay in a newspaper, journal, or magazine

Atlas   A book of maps

Autobiography   An account that a person writes about his or her own life; a memoir

Bibliography   A list of books and articles on a specific subject

Biography   A written account of a person's life

Book review index   A listing of book reviews that have appeared in journals, magazines, and newspapers

Bound periodicals   A number of issues of journals or magazines bound together with a hard cover

Call number   The identification number that tells where to find a book on the library shelf; books and periodicals are arranged by call number

Card catalog   Drawers with cards arranged alphabetically by author, title, and subject listing all the books in the library; each card has information about the book and the call number to help locate the book

CD-ROM (Compact disk with read-only memory)   A laser disk that can hold the equivalent of 1500 floppy disks; many periodical indexes are available on CD-ROM

Checkout   The procedure for borrowing a book from the library

Circulating   A book that can be checked out of the library

Circulation desk   The area where you check out books, renew books, return books, pay fines for overdue books, place holds on books, and recall books

Closed stacks   Stacks closed to students. When a book is requested, a librarian gets it from the shelf.

Computer search   The search through a database for books and articles on a particular topic

Computerized catalog   An on-line system that lists all the books in the library collection by author, title, and subject, giving information about the book and the call number to help a student locate it. In many libraries, this system is replacing the card catalog.

Copyright   The legal right given to an author or publisher for exclusive publication and distribution

Dewey decimal system   A system of classification still used in some small, older libraries in the United States

Dictionary   A book containing lists of words, meanings, pronunciation, usage, and etymology of words. There are general and specialized dictionaries.

Due date   The date stamped inside a book when it is checked out of the library indicating when it must be returned

Encyclopedia   A collection of articles written by specialists and arranged in alphabetical order by subject. There are general and specialized encyclopedias, and they often contain bibliographies.

Etymology   The origin and historical development of a word

Fact books   Almanacs, yearbooks, and statistical abstracts

Fiction   A literary work that is not based on fact but came from the writer's imagination

Fine   The amount of money that has to be paid each day if a book is returned after the due date

Folio   A large book; folios are often shelved in a separate area of the library

Government publications   A collection of publications from the federal government, the state government, and possibly other governmental organizations such as the United Nations

Hold   After filling out a form at the circulation desk, a librarian will notify you when a book has been returned to the library and will keep it for you for a specified number of days

Index   References to articles from journals, magazines, and newspapers, arranged alphabetically by subject; periodical index

Index tables   Tables in the reference area where indexes are shelved

Interlibrary loan   Borrowing books through your library from another library

Journal   A publication containing articles on scholarly research

Librarian   A person trained in library science

Library of Congress   The national library of the United States in Washington D.C., founded in 1800

Library of Congress classification system   The system of classification used in most university libraries in which books are grouped together by subject, and each book is given a call number

Library of Congress subject headings (LCSH)   A complete list of terms used in the Library of Congress system of classification

Literature   Imaginative or creative writing in prose or verse

Magazine   A publication containing articles on popular or general subjects

Manuscript   A handwritten composition; the author's own handwritten or typewritten copy of a book, article, etc.

Maps   A representation of a region of the earth

Media   A means of mass communication: newspapers, magazines, television, etc.

Memoir   An account that a person writes about his or her own life; an autobiography

Microfiche   A 4" x 6" sheet of film with a series of micro-images

Microfilm   A roll of film with a series of micro-images

Microform   Photographic film with micro-images, often used to store periodicals and archival material

Noncirculating   Not be taken out of the library (referring to certain books or other materials)

Nonfiction   A literary work based on fact; not fiction

On-line   In a computer system

Open stacks   Stacks open to students, who can go to the shelves and get books without the assistance of a librarian

Overdue   Not returned to the library by the due date (referring to books or other circulating materials)

Pamphlet   A short, unbound printed work with a paper cover

Periodical   A publication that is published regularly—daily, weekly, monthly, etc.

Periodical index   References to articles found in periodicals, listed alphabetically by subject

Periodical printout   A listing of all periodicals held by a library; serial printout

Publication date   The year a book is put in print

Readers' Guide to Periodical Literature   An index of nearly 200 periodicals of general interest

Reference area   An area of the library that contains encyclopedias, dictionaries, factbooks, directories, and other sources containing practical and specific information

Reference books   Encyclopedias, dictionaries, factbooks, directories, and other sources containing practical and specific information

Reference desk   A section of the reference area where librarians are available to assist you

Reference stacks   Shelves holding noncirculating reference sources

Renew   Check out a book again that you currently have. You can only do this if no one else has placed a hold on it.

Reserve book room   An area where professors place books and articles for students to check out for short periods of time

Reshelving area   A holding area for books in the library that have not yet been put back on the shelves in proper call-number order

Serial printout   A listing of all periodicals held by a library; periodical printout

Special collection   A collection of rare books, manuscripts, archives, etc.

Stacks   The shelves that hold the library's books and bound periodicals

Statistical abstract   An annual publication with lists, charts, and tables of global statistics and facts

Study carrel A small private study area in the stacks of a library

Style manual   A book that gives writing rules and examples used to prepare research papers, dissertations, and articles for publication; available in the general reference area

Unabridged   Having the original length; not shortened or condensed (e.g., an unabridged dictionary)

Yearbook   An annual publication with lists, charts, and tables of information about the previous year